West Virginia Glass
Between the World Wars

Dean Six

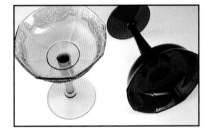

Schiffer Publishing Ltd

4880 Lower Valley Road, Atglen, PA 19310 USA

Dedicated to my parents,
Ralph Kester Six and Eleanor L. McGinnis Six their love and support has never failed

Library of Congress Cataloging-in-Publication Data

Six, Dean.
West Virginia glass between the world wars / by Dean Six.
p. cm.
ISBN 0-7643-1546-3
1. Glassware--West Virginia--History--20th century. 2. Glass manufacture--West Virginia--History--20th century. I. Title: West Virginia glass. II. Title.
NK5112 .S56 2002
748.29154"09"041--dc21
2001006599

Designed by Bonnie M. Hensley
Cover design by Bruce M. Waters
Type set in Mona Lisa Recut/Lydian BT

ISBN: 0-7643-1546-3
Printed in China
1 2 3 4

Published by Schiffer Publishing Ltd.
4880 Lower Valley Road
Atglen, PA 19310
Phone: (610) 593-1777; Fax: (610) 593-2002
E-mail: Schifferbk@aol.com
Please visit our web site catalog at **www.schifferbooks.com**

In Europe, Schiffer books are distributed by Bushwood Books
6 Marksbury Avenue Kew Gardens
Surrey TW9 4JF England
Phone: 44 (0) 20-8392-8585; Fax: 44 (0) 20-8392-9876
E-mail: Bushwd@aol.com
Free postage in the UK. Europe: air mail at cost.

This book may be purchased from the publisher.
Include $3.95 for shipping. Please try your bookstore first.
We are always looking for people to write books on new and related subjects.
If you have an idea for a book please contact us at the above address.
You may write for a free catalog.

Contents

Acknowledgments 4

Introduction 5

    Sharing 5

    Pricing 5

    How It All Began 5

Alley Glass Co. 7

Beaumont Glass 10

Blenko Glass 15

Bonita Glass 17

Central Glass Works 19

Columbia Glass Co. 33

Dunbar Glass 34

Fenton Art Glass 46

Fostoria 52

Hazel Atlas 57

Huntington Tumbler 63

Louie Glass Co. 69

Mid-Atlantic 78

Monongah Glass Co. 79

Morgantown Glassware Guild 89

New Martinsville Glass 98

Paden City 108

Paramount Glass 121

Seneca Glass 123

Vitrolite 138

Westite Glass 140

Weston Glass Co. 147

West Virginia Glass Specialty 152

Index 160

Acknowledgments

One of my favorite African proverbs says it takes an entire village to raise a child. So it is with some books. This is such a book and it has required several villages to get this far! For well over two decades I have worked this information over and over. I have presented portions of this material to numerous glass clubs and national glass conventions, and learned from each experience. If you helped me, as so many have, please hear my sincere thanks. Some, certainly not all, who merit my appreciation include: Dr. Emory Kemp, Merle Moore, Frank Fenton, Eason Eige, Holly McClusky, Don Smith, Jaime Robinson, Dave Bush and Sally Lockard, Rock Wilson, Roy and Doris White, Bob Page, Dale Frederiksen, the late French Batten, Jim Marshall, Kelsey Murphy, Anne Madarasz, Tom and Neila Bredehoft, Jeff Conover, MWV, Tim Schmidt, Michael & Susie, JoAnne and Earl Autenreith, my parents Eleanor and Kester Six, and certainly my faithful and loving grandmother, June McGinnis.

Introduction

Sharing

Some of the glass shown in this book is from the collection of the West Virginia Museum of American Glass, Ltd. on Main Avenue in Weston, West Virginia. To the Museum I am grateful for the privilege of including images from that collection and for other kindness, support, and benefits over time. I strongly encourage anyone with an interest in twentieth century American glass to visit, join, correspond with, or otherwise connect with this small but dynamic institution at P.O. Box 574 Weston, WV 26452. I am not without bias, having been involved with the museum since its inception. In addition to the Museum collection, people from the Weston Area Glass Study Group carried in pieces from their private collections to be included in this book. Such sharing is a gift of kindness of considerable magnitude. I thank the following, both on my behalf and on behalf of readers for years to come: John and Susie Determan, Roy and Doris White, Susie Thayer, Bill Law, Nelson Linger and Casey, & Dave Bush.

Pricing

I have struggled to include suggested prices for the objects I have selected to show. This was far more difficult for me than any other part of this book project. First let me share the standard warning that these are only suggestions of possible price ranges. The prices printed herein are not definite answers to value but my judgment on actual market place value and only that. Let me also add that I have long raged against books that set unrealistically high values and expect the market to then catch up to those printed numbers. I find this unethical and deceptive practice to hurt the hobby of glass collecting and antiques in general. The suggested price ranges in this text seek to reflect, but may at times miss, the price pieces shown sell for. I attend auctions, shop the market and web, and price glass for resale, in part, for a living. I can with absolute honesty say the prices included herein represent what I believe to be a real and actual current price at which these objects sell in the places where I live and work. You should use judgment and undertake some exploration where you buy to confirm that these price trends apply there as well.

How It All Began

For several years I have wanted to write this book.

I wanted to write about the glass that excited me, the firey liquid that cools to an endless array of colors. I wanted to tell a part of the story of an industry that had surrounded me as a child growing up in West Virginia. I wanted to tell the world that there was more, much more, to my much loved state than coal. And I wanted to share a bit of the extensive collection of objects and history I have gathered in over a decade of chasing the lesser known stories of West Virginia's Glass Industry.

West Virginia began to make glass years before it separated from Virginia in 1863. Perhaps as early as 1813 glass was being made in Wellsburg, West Virginia (then known as Charles Town, Virginia). In quality and style the earliest products resembled what was then being made in Pittsburgh or "back east".

Available fuel, in this case coal, and transportation to the west via the Ohio River had drawn early glass makers to West Virginia. The same reasons would reoccur again and again over the decades to come.

As the 1800s gave way to the 1900s, changes came about that made West Virginia a major glass producer.

Many major events occurred in the glass industry between 1890 and the 1910s. A West Virginian, Michael Owens, invented a mechanical bottle blowing machine that revolutionized bottle manufacture first and, later, adaptations in that technology made possible inexpensive machine made tableware (collector's "depression glass"). Window glass, a little known but very large portion of the glass industry in the early 1900s, was transformed from a labor intensive handmade, mouth blown product to a machine made product. Dozens of window glass factories closed, thousand of skilled glass workers' jobs were lost by the late 1920s. Other innovations continued to make changes in how we made glass.

The most significant factor influencing what is today collectable glass from the first half of the twentieth century was the discovery of natural gas in large and dependable quantities in West Virginia.

Oil had been drilled for in West Virginia before the Civil War. Natural gas was known to exist but the ability to transport and use it safely took time to develop. By the turn of the twentieth century, and shortly thereafter, glass factories that had been founded in or moved into Indiana, parts of Ohio, and other westward locations had suffered greatly from the failure of the natural gas supply. Many companies became insolvent and closed. Some relocated to West Virginia. The first decades of the twentieth century found an ever increasing number of glass factories producing in West Virginia. This number grew until it peaked in the mid-1920s.

The decline in the number of window glass plants mentioned above and the world wide economic conditions around 1930 account for the reversal and decline of the West Virginia glass industry. This is the stage, in the broadest historical context, that opens West Virginia to being a major national and world glass producer in the period between the world wars.

For the purpose of this book I shall loosely define the period "between the world wars" as from the beginning of World War I in 1914 to the end of World War II in 1945. These dates and the phrase "between the wars" are only rough guidelines. The glass industry, individual companies, and types of production did not react in neat and concise ways to historical dates. Trends in glass may last a few months and fade or linger for many decades. I chose the war time dates because they give most of us some sense of a large and specific block of time and because it was during these decades that the glass industry in West Virginia grew significantly, producing the greatest variety of wares. It is also when many glass companies came into being and vanished, the companies that may have been giants in their day but are little known today. These are the companies and the products that most fascinate me and this is their time.

As I began to collect glass for myself and later for the West Virginia Museum of American Glass, Ltd. It became increasingly clear that the companies' products that I frequently found were not the subject of the dozens of collector books I knew of. These products were often exquisite examples of color, craft, form and design, and innovation. Yet they were mentioned in no, or very few, printed sources. These were sleeping giants, forgotten short-lived minor players and some "not-so-minor-in-their-day" players. Sometimes the products were lesser known early lines of later successful companies. Thus, this book project was born and nurtured.

I will detail some of this later in specific chapter but what I found and continue to find amazes me. An example would be a full page advertisement dated February 23, 1910 for a New York glass showroom, Frank N. Miller. The top of the page illustrates "The Monongah Glass Co. of Fairmont, W.Va.: pressed and blown, stemware, tumblers and tableware, in needle etchings, enamel decorations, sand blast and cut. Jelly Tumblers, beer mugs, etc". Wow. Amazing variety. But the really amazing part is the "other" company in the ad: "The H. Northwood Glass Co. of Wheeling, W.Va." The Northwood copy mentions specific colors or patterns. Monongah illustrates a panel and wheel hand cut and mouth blown jug (pitcher) and matching tumbler. Northwood shows a pressed fruit bowl. What I read from this ad is that Monongah was the "Top" line, got top billing, and offered a type of ware that would have been more expensive. Northwood offered a variety of pressed wares. But, today Northwood is well known and Monongah all but forgotten. To support my argument of which was the larger glass house at the time, Northwood employees rarely, if ever, numbered over a few hundred. Monongah employed as many as 650 in their glass production and maintained three production sites. It is this type of re-consideration I seek to inspire us all to. I in no way wish to belittle the products of the genius Harry Northwood, nor can I accept a glass history that neglect so many factories and stories that were, in their day, "Top of The Line."

Why has this view of glass and the glass industry's history evolved whereby we elevate a few and forget the many? In the past is has often been a focus on the men who were giants, captains of the industry, that has been told as glass history. Furthermore, collectors have been the driving forces behind, and have sometimes written, many of the existing glass histories. Harry Northwood is an example. He and his products are well known today because of the production of iridescent or "carnival" glass. Carnival became hotly collected in the late 1960s and books soon followed. Northwood, and much Carnival glass, was pressed pattern glass. Such glass, once you learn the patterns, is not terribly difficult as to attribution and thus collecting is easier. The types of glass we have collected are the types of glass about which books are published, the glass people can learn to identify and seek. Carnival, depression glass, Fostoria, Fenton, kitchen glass, bedroom and bath glass, etc. As more collectors appear and available glass becomes scarcer and/or more expensive, we want to learn about other related products.

It is my hope that this book will be a tool to broaden the understanding of glass production. I further accept some responsibility for introducing and identifying glassware lines for collectors that have been long overlooked. I ask you not to forget that many of the companies in this text were indeed well known and respected in their day. Many of these were successful for long periods of time. It has been the ease of access to information and the collector-driven desires for certain types of information that has popularized certain types of glass. Finding great amounts of information on lesser known companies can range from difficult to neigh impossible. Did the availability of photo price guides drive the depression glass market or did the demand for information on depression glass produce the books? It is likely a chicken and egg question, but clearly information on the dozens and, literally, dozens of Other Glass Companies is needed. This is not the final word. Many West Virginia glass companies are not mentioned; not because of their inferior product but because so little is yet known about them.

In this tome I offer you a series of essays on lesser-known glass producers. The essays reflect a wide diversity in the type of information given. The essays are as different as the products these companies once offered!

I offer you essays telling parts of the stories of over twenty West Virginia glass companies. Some of your favorites companies may not be featured in depth. It seems my reasons for writing would be lost if I attempted to tell you something new about Fostoria Glass, or Fenton Glass, or some of the others about which much has been written. To remind us that some of those very popular and recognized companies were (or are) in West Virginia and were in fact the competitors for the concerns discussed here, I have included brief mention of them and provide a short bibliography on where to find more information. Look there and explore other possible sources.

This is the story of a few of The Other West Virginia Glass Companies within a very specific time period. Each is its own story, an essay about one company. The essays and the companies are as individualistic as you and me. Enjoy.

Alley Glass Co.

If Lawrence (L. E.) Alley had made only glass marbles it is likely the company would still have merited a mention here. However, as we learn of production, including glass children's dishes long attributed to the Akro Agate Glass Co. and others, along with the presence of numerous small vases and other pressed glass articles, it became evident that the Alley story merited some attention; in fact, this story needs to be told here.

Alley, like numerous other glass men, had connections to many places and worked with some of the giants in the industry. His family relates that he began work in glass at the age of eighteen or nineteen at Fostoria Glass as a carry-in boy, a no-skill beginning position. By 1910, Alley was working at Huntington Glass in Huntington, West Virginia, and maybe that was where he learned to cut glass. When Huntington Glass closed, he went to Fenton and was a cutter there circa 1914-1915. His glass journey had begun.

So unfolds this story of one glass man, L. E. Alley. The story is not unique but very typical of roving glass workers. Alley appears in the written glass industry records of West Virginia in 1917 when he is listed in the National Glass Budget Directory as General Manager and Vice President of Kingwood Glass Co, in Kingwood, West Virginia. This short-lived company (circa 1917-1921) made "blown tumblers, stemware and light cut glass". By 1919, Alley was no longer listed as an officer for this company. He returned to Fenton and cut glass there for about a year before relocating to St. Mary's, West Virginia, as a cutter for a company there. He next worked in Cumberland, Maryland, then moved to Shinnston, West Virginia, to act as general manager of Pacquet Glass.

Marble lore tells that Alley began his career as a "gathering boy" at marble giant, Akro Agate, in Clarksburg, West Virginia. Perhaps. However, Akro Agate did not move to Clarksburg until 1914 and it seems unlikely a carry in boy of 1914 is a Vice President and General Manager in 1917. Furthermore, his moves and jobs left little time for such a side trip, it might be argued. His family suggests Alley worked in some capacity at Akro shortly prior to 1930.

Returning to the trail, Alley next surfaced in glass literature in 1922 in Shinnston, West Virginia. *China, Glass and Lamps* (CG & L) magazine of October 30, 1922 reported "L. E. Alley of the Alley Glass Co. of Shinnston, W.Va., and Harry Gilbert, a factory engineer of Bridgeport Conn., are reported to be the moving spirits behind a plan to erect a glass factory to cost $300,000 at Shinnston. The new factory would be connected with the present factory of Alley Glass Co., which manufactures

stemware and tumblers . . ." It seems likely the factory never materialized, as a report in *China, Glass & Lamps* a short time later states that the factory of Alley Glass Co., "cut glass manufacturers of Shinnston, W. Va., has moved to the old Baptist church in Shinnston. Operations will resume . . . with 20 cutting frames . . .," a cutting frame being one work station in the process of hand cutting glass. The works in Shinnston lasted until about 1924, when it is noted in the State of West Virginia Board of Labor report. In Shinnston, there were perhaps three operating glass manufacturers in the early 1920s, so Alley had ample suppliers for his cutting blanks. Can any of us identify any of the products from these factories or cutting shops? It is unlikely.

By 1928, Alley Glass Co. is listed in the *National Glass Budget Directory* (NGBD) in Salem, West Virginia, his Shinnston firm having somehow merged with an existing Salem concern. No officers are listed and production is the ever uncertain "small glass novelties." I can find no other data on the Salem production. Is it possible that this production included children's glass dishes? It is a part of local lore in Pennsboro, West Virginia, where Alley would also appear, that he came to Pennsboro from Salem.

Alley's first recorded presence in Pennsboro is in 1935, as cited in the *Glass Factory Yearbook & Directory*. A listing appears for "Alley Agate Co., Pennsboro, W.Va." with "L. E. Alley, owner."

I believe Alley came to Pennsboro because a site that had been built for two hand blown window glass factories sat idle and unused. This site, locally know as "glass factory hollow," today remains home to Champion Agate and, until 1997, was also the location of Pennsboro Glass Co. This long lineage of glass in the same location gives rise to the importance attached to existing natural gas, workers, machinery, buildings, or some combination thereof.

That Alley made children's dishes at this Pennsboro site cannot be questioned. Locally it was referred to as "the dish factory," not a marble factory as the Agate name implies. I have listened to several elderly ladies report on passing the site as youths when an adult presented them with toy dishes from the cullet piles. Another lady shared her story of being given a set of boxed child's glass dishes when she visited the site. Today, earthen fill and a newer building obscure any discoveries at the site. Alley appears to have been active in Pennsboro until 1948.

During some of this same time Lawrence Glass & Novelty Co. is operating in Sistersville, West Virginia! As early as 1931 find the Lawrence company in *NGBD* with L. E. Alley, owner. In 1932 Berry Pink, a name to later play a dominate role in the marble business, is added to the Lawrence Glass & Novelty Co. officers as "treasurer and purchasing agent." West Virginia Department of Labor reports note the company operating in Sistersville as late as 1938 with less than 25 employees.

Alley is reported in secondary sources to have operated a factory in Paden City, West Virginia, beginning in 1929. It is said to have been in or near the old Paul Wismach glass plant and it is told that it was here that Pink joined the firm. With the interest in collecting marbles increasing, the story of a child's glass dish maker and marble manufacturer of amazing stamina and resilience merits much greater research.

Dun & Bradstreet include a report on Alley Manufacturing Company in 1948. The Alley Glass Manufacturing Co. of St. Marys, West Virginia, is listed in *The Glass Factory Yearbook* for 1949 as a producer of toy marbles, toy dishes, and glass novelties in color and color combinations. Their production facilities included seven continuous tanks and two day tanks. Continuous tanks are large "cooking furnaces" for making glass. Raw materials are repeatedly added at one end as production continues at the other, creating a "continuous tank" of hot glass. Day tanks are smaller furnaces that are filled with a single batch of glass, roughly enough to support one day's production. Without knowing how large those continuous tanks were, seven tanks translates into the ability to produce a great deal of glass!

Production of small colored opaque children's dishes, vases, and "novelties" have long been attributed to the Alley company in St. Mary's. Examples dug at the site, including some in the collection of the West Virginia Museum of American Glass, Ltd., and various ex-employees verify the production. For years, there has been much debate over certain children's dishes attributed to Akro Agate of Clarksburg, West Virginia. Evidence suggests that dishes of particular colors, patterns, and markings may well have been produced by a firm other than Akro Agate. Many of the children's dishes, including many once attributed to Akro Agate, bear the mark "J.P." on their reverse. Serious students of Akro Agate glass have long questioned the difference in quality of pressing found on marked Akro dishes and the dishes bearing the J.P. mark. Akro Agate experts and authors Claudia and Roger Hardy report that in their years of digging at the old Akro site **in Clarksburg, West Virginia**, NO pieces of glass with the "J.P." mark were discovered. The Hardys recovered thousands and thousands of shards from the Akro site, making the sheer "weight" of the evidence overwhelming that the J.P. marked pieces are not Akro.

The J.P. mark represents the firm J. Pressman, a New York toy company for whom glass children's dishes and Chinese checker sets with marbles were a giant success. It can be documented that Alley made marbles for J. Pressman's Chinese Checker boards. Is this a possible reason to link the two business associates together in the glass dishes business as well? A final piece of this puzzle comes from the late Dr. Bud Appleton, the author

of one of the earliest Akro Agate texts. He stated to the crowd at the Akro Collectors Convention a few years back that he had originally surmised the J.P. pieces to be Akro and thus included them in his early book. He went on and reported he no longer believed this. For now, I urge us to follow his lead and to attribute all "J.P." glass child's dishes to Lawrence Alley, at St. Mary's, West Virginia, and possibly at some of his several other factories, and to no longer call them Akro Agate.

The career of L. E. Alley, and the impact of his traveling presence, left an imprint on many West Virginia glass towns and on many people who would later be engaged in glass. His influence was so great that rumors of his involvement in other glass towns persist. Whether these rumors are fed by truth or by his reputation we cannot say. Reports of his involvement in glass businesses in the towns of Ravenswood and Parkersburg/Vienna keep surfacing. The complete extent and impact of Lawrence Alley will never be known, but we can say with certainty he was a major influence and factor in the decades between the world wars. The Alley factory in St. Mary's was sold in 1949 and became Marble King.

Alley Glass Co. small bakers, 3 ½ inches, $8-12 each. Note variations in green from opaque to transparent, common in Alley products. *West Virginia Museum of American Glass collection.*

Alley Glass Co. miniature flower pots, 1 ¼ inches diameter each: opaque green with no embossing, $14-20; blue and white embossed on bottom "Braum & Corwin", $50-60. Some sold as part of dime store child's craft set with flowers to glue into pots, etc. *West Virginia Museum of American Glass collection.*

Alley Glass Co. garden dish with panel side and scalloped rim, opaque green, 1 ¼ inches, 7 inches in length, $12-18. Child's or individual casserole with tab lid, opaque green, 4 ½ inches diameter, $14-20. *West Virginia Museum of American Glass collection.*

Alley Glass Co. child's "Toy Dishes" set in original box, opaque green, unmarked. Note original 35 cent purchase price. $100-120. *West Virginia Museum of American Glass collection.*

Alley Glass Co. children's dishes: cobalt ringed tab handled tea cup, no mark, 1 ½ inches, $6-8; amber tea pot with tab handle, "J.P." embossed on bottom, 2 ¾ inches, $20-24; opaque purple tab handled tea cup, embossed "J.P." on bottom, 1 ½ inches with saucer, $14-22; opaque blue tab handled cream, embossed "J.P." on bottom, 1 ½ inches, $12-16.

Beaumont Glass

The story of the Beaumont Glass Co. relates well as the story of a single man. Percy J. Beaumont was a native of England who came to Wheeling, West Virginia, in 1882, being then eighteen years of age. Percy's only sister married Harry Northwood, another Englishman whose influence on American and West Virginia glass was great. One can only imagine the family conversations when these two titans of glass were together!

Briefly outlined, Percy Beaumont organized the Beaumont Glass Co. in Martin's Ferry, Ohio, in 1890; when this concern outgrew its quarters in 1902, he relocated his company to Grafton, West Virginia. In 1905 he sold his interest in the Grafton factory, a producer of hand blown tableware, to become manager of The Union Stopper Company of Morgantown, West Virginia. Union Stopper made non-refillable stoppers of glass for whiskey bottles. This odd sounding product "flopped almost immediately, whereupon the facilities of the new plant were given over to the manufacturer of tableware in 1906 and P. J. (our Percy) Beaumont joined the company as manager."(The Glass Industry Vol. 20 No. 2 Feb. 1939). Union Stopper introduced blown "illuminating ware" in 1912 and in 1915 was busy enough to require the purchasing of another glass plant, the closed Wrightman Bottle factory in Sabraton, West Virginia, a small town near Morgantown. A dated 1915 price list in the Corning Museum of Glass lists over 200 variations on ink wells and desk accessories in the Union Stopper line. In 1917 Union Stopper became the Beaumont Company, manufacturers of "illuminated glassware and stationers' sundries." That loosely translates into light globes, light shades, and ink wells. (History of West Virginia Old and New. The American Historical Society 1923 and Timberland Trails Vol. 2 no. 3 1958) Beaumont products of this period include those not widely exciting to most collectors.

Unfortunately, chasing the product from this sizeable factory over the decades is more difficult than ascertaining who was factory manager! Beaumont has long been a "sleeper" in the glass world. During my tenure as a university student in Morgantown I frequently encountered town resident's who had never heard of Beaumont Glass, right there in their own town! Little wonder the company is a mystery yet today in glass and antiques circles.

It is known that a Georgian pattern was produced by Beaumont. I saw a yellowed two page illustrated Beaumont catalogue spread of Georgian pattern Beaumont pasted on the walls of the factory in the 1980s. No copy of this catalog has been found.

A line that haunted glass historian William Heacock was an opaque white color he called "moonstone" or "clambroth" glass. Heacock, a respected glass writer, illustrated two pieces with hand decoration and listed them as "made by the mystery manufacturer" in one of his early glass magazines. Today this color of glass is known to be Fer-Lux, a glass developed for use in lighting fixtures. The name and attribution for this type of glass goes to The Union Stopper Company, later Beaumont, and can be dated to an early 1915 Pottery, Glass and Brass Salesman advertisement. The Fer-Lux glass was used in a tableware line of hexagon shape, novelties, and perhaps other lines. A similar Beaumont glass is an opaque jade green. Beaumont's octagonal tableware line can be found in this green as well as the Fer-Lux.

We can learn of some of the Beaumont production line from pieces given to the Huntington Museum of Art in Huntington, West Virginia, by Arthur Beaumont himself, son of the founder and for many years factory manager. These pieces include several with large dots or polka dots on white opaque glass.

The Beaumont Company remained largely in the hands of the two families who had shaped the company in its earliest years: the grandson of company founder, Richard A. Canfield and Beaumont's son, Arthur, until 1978. Beaumont remained a major producer of lamp and lighting ware until its closing in (1993). Today the factory has been razed and nothing marks the spot where glass was made for almost a century. Hand painting, cased glass, tortoise shell, and other highly skilled products appeared in the Beaumont line in the decades after World War II, making it a company worthy of greater research and interest.

Beaumont Glass Co. variations from one mold for three toed bowls. Opaque white with hand painted small floral with gold rim; opaque hand painted larger floral opaque green, with gold rim; opaque with silver band, all 2 ³⁄₄ inches tall, $15-25 each.

Powder box, Beaumont Glass Co., octagonal powder box with lid bottom embossed in oval "Royal Furniture Co. Morgantown, W.Va.", opaque/jade green, 4 ½ inches diameter, $50-65.

Line 148, Beaumont Glass Co. All opaque white. Six sided cream and sugar, octagonal sugar with red polka dot decoration, all 4 inches to top of handle, $15-20 each and six sided saucer with red polka dot decoration, 5 ¾ inches. Saucer requires tea cup, not sugar bowl, $5-8.

Beaumont Glass Co. Four toed ruby console bowl, 12 ½ inches at handles, $60-80. *Gift of Joyce Clark in memory of her grandmother, Elizabeth Hayes. West Virginia Museum of American Glass collection.*

Console bowl, Beaumont Glass Co. Four toed opaque white, 12 ½ inches, $35-45.

Fan vase, Beaumont Glass Co. Opaque white,
7 ½ inches, $28-38.

Cornucopias, Beaumont Glass Co. Both opaque white. Cornucopia vases, 6 ¼ inches, $30-40; cornucopia candleholders with silver deposit decoration (tarnished), 4 ½ inches, $35-45.

Beaumont Glass Co. Both opaque white. Box with lid, 3 inches to finial top, $30-40; tonic or bitters bottle, 6 ½ inches, $15-25. The bottle is similar to a Fenton form and possibly others. This example has a good Morgantown provenance, however, and thus my tentative attribution.

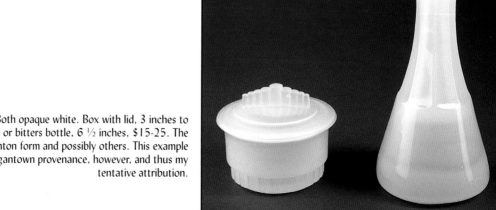

Candy Jar #20, Beaumont Glass Co., covered candy jar/urn form. Hand painted chintz decoration and gold banding, 10 inches, $45-55.

Vase, Beaumont Glass Co. Four toed base, 2 ½ inches tall, flared vase with gold star decoration, opaque white, 6 ¼ inches, $50-65.

Console set, Beaumont Glass Co. No. 115 bowl, 12 ½ inches, $45-55; open single light candlestick, opaque white, 5 ¼ inches, $25-35 each.

Line 148 cake plates or serving trays, Beaumont Glass Co. Six sided, two open handled trays, green decoration, $35-45, and red decoration, $35-45. Both opaque white, 13 ½ inches tip handle to handle

Basket No. 682, Beaumont Glass Co. Basket vase or "ice bucket," all opaque white. Chintz mini-floral decoration, hand painted, worn gold trim, $40-50 in good condition; black polka dots and gold banding decoration with gold handles, $30-40; hand painted floral decoration and russet handles, $45-55 as shown. All 6 inches tall at handles.

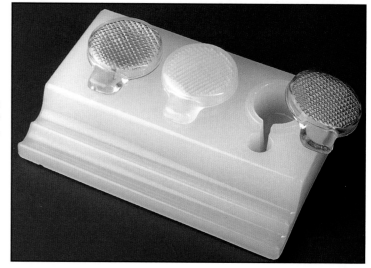

Ink well, Beaumont Glass Co. Three well ink stand/base with pen rest and three covers for black, blue, and red inks. Opaque white and clear glass, 6 ¾ inches, $50- 65.

Paperweight, Beaumont Glass Co. Figural horse head paperweight, clear, 3 ¾ inches, $40-50.

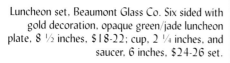

Luncheon set, Beaumont Glass Co. Six sided with gold decoration, opaque green/jade luncheon plate, 8 ½ inches, $18-22; cup, 2 ¼ inches, and saucer, 6 inches, $24-26 set.

Blenko Glass

A third-generation, family-owned glass company, Blenko has its origins in a quest for recreating the bright colors of English cathedral window glass. While the company continues today to be a world leader in making flat glass for leaded and stained glass, a decision in the 1930s to combat tough financial times led to producing tableware. To most students of glass, Blenko's is the long history of designer conscious, handcrafted tableware and decorative vessels that are know and recognized. The use of the bold colors developed for light filtering windows remains a strong point of Blenko production in the Milton, West Virginia, factory.

Many Blenko forms appear timeless. This may be due, in part, to the use of organic glass shapes, shapes wherein the natural flow of hot liquid glass and gravity aid in forming an object's shape. Blenko's use of simple wooden molds, devoid of excessive pattern, further aids in producing a fluid appearing shape and one that may be repeated over time. The wooden molds burn out and are recreated, only to burn out again and again. This use of a form over time, coupled with reintroduction of shapes, places some popular Blenko forms on the market for decades. This is not unique to Blenko, but coupled with their hand formed methods it often makes the dating of a piece complex. Color is often the key. I believe the pieces illustrated to be all of the proper period. There remains much to learn about the early decades of Blenko production.

In recent years the more Modern design influenced Blenko has attracted attention and several Blenko books have been written on mid-century production. Only one work deals with the early period between the wars. For a detailed history and extensive photos of early production seek:

Eige, Eason and Rick Wilson. *Blenko Glass 1930-1953*. Marietta, Ohio: Antique Publications, 1987.

Tumbler, Blenko Glass Co. Blue with applied berry prunts, rough pontiled, 5 ½ inches. $28-34.

Blenko Glass Co. Vase, rimmed, aqua optic with rough pontil, 5 ½ inches, $34-42; vase, aqua, heavily seeded, rough pontiled, 8 ¼ inches, $45-55; bowl, green, seeded, and rough pontiled, irregular sheared rim, 5 inches, $38-48. Note: the pontil mark is the rough scar on the object's base where it was once attached to an iron rod for handling when hot.

Blenko Glass Co. flip vase, amber green, 9 ¼ inches, rough pontiled. $20-30. *Rock Wilson Collection.*

Blenko Glass Co. tableware. All rough pontiled, with seeds/bubbles throughout. Circa 1930s. Footed tumbler, 5 ¼ inches, $14-16; footed juice, 3 inches, $8-12; luncheon plate with rolled rim, 7 ¾ inches, $14-16; sherbet or dessert bowl, 2 ½ inches, $12-14. *Rock Wilson collection.*

Blenko Glass Co. Tumbler, ruby with hand applied prunts and rough pontil, 5 ½ inches, $35-48; fan vase, clear crackle vase with green applied rose prunts and foot, rough pontil and applied prunts, 9 ¼ inches, $45-55; tumbler, small hand applied prunts near base blue with rough pontil, 5 ½ inches, $16-24.

Blenko Glass Co. punch set. Green, heavily seeded, punch cups with hand applied handles, 2 ½ inches. 8 ¼ inches x 9 ¼ inches diameter with ladle, all rough pontiled. Set with 12 cups (only 4 shown) $280-360. *Rock Wilson collection.*

Blenko crackled crystal with color ad from the Robert P. Pierce Merchandise Mart, Chicago, Illinois.

Bonita Glass

The story of Bonita Glass reads like a detective novel. "Who done its" and clue seeking cloak the history of this fairly long-lived, often traveling glass company.

The constant factor in most of the Bonita story is one man: Otto Jaeger. Jaeger learned glass engraving as a youth and for many years was an officer and general manager of the Bonita Art Glass Co. of Wheeling, West Virginia. Earlier in his life, in 1877, he accepted employment at Hobbs, Brockunier Glass in Wheeling and there took charge of the cutting, etching, and engraving departments of this then industry leader. He was twenty-four years old. Jeager was one of the organizers of Fostoria Glass in 1888 and in 1891 was president of the newly organized Seneca Glass Co. In 1899 he was operating a factory in Cicero, Indiana, called The Bonita Glass Co., working with Charles Hobbs. By 1901, he had returned to Wheeling and formed the Bonita Art Glass Co., of which he served as secretary, treasurer, and general manager. For years the business was primarily a decorator of china and glass employing 100 persons.

In 1919, the *China and Glass Journal* (4 October) tells us "the Bonita Art Co., whose line is shown in New York by Cox & Lafferty, 1140 Broadway, are certainly doing things these days. Every month brings something new from this concern. Among the very latest additions to the line are several clever conceptions in transparent rose patterns on lemonade, water and grape juice sets, and a very dainty cluster of grape design in natural colors especially for the latter. There is also an octagonal-shaped covered salad bowl with a continuous wild flower decoration that is very dainty." Also in 1919 we read of "some remarkable treatments . . . in blown, stem and flat ware. The gold decorated ware is very attractive, and the tinted band decorations on the stem and blown goods are striking features . . ."

While it has been argued that Bonita was "only" a decorator during the Wheeling years period, literatures suggests otherwise. The 1920 *China, Glass and Lamp Directory* lists "Bonita Art Co., Wheeling, W.Va." Officers were Geo. E. House, President; Otto Jaeger, Secretary, Treasurer, General Manager and Sales Manager and with the company having "two day tanks with eight rings." This information affirms that there was hot glass production capacity and how large it was . . . eight rings could support eight shops of glass workers and be a medium-sized production facility. We may conclude that Bonita, in circa 1919-1920, was a decorator on china, on their own glass, as well as on glass products by other concerns.

By the 1920s Bonita and Jaeger have relocated to Huntington, West Virginia. The firm was certainly, according to trade advertisements, a decorating house using china and glass. But several snippets of information again suggest or imply that hot glass production was part of the operation shortly after relocation. One prime and intriguing passage is found in the *Crockery and Glass Journal*, January 8, 1927 "After an illness of nearly three months, caused by his having been struck by an automobile, Otto Jaeger, of the Bonita Art Glass Co. of Huntington, W.Va. is again able to be at his desk." He would have been sixty-four years old then.

This amazing trade journal quote continues:

This concern is showing for this special season several new lines, one of them being of Peach Blow order, a copy of a vase that was sold nearly a half century ago for $15,000. This particular vase stood eight inches in height. A similar line was made by the old firm of Hobbs, Brockunier & Co. of Wheeling, W.Va. high in price and at that time had an excellent sale. But, at that time, the line was made of case glass, and the manufacturers not being familiar enough to have the two glasses agree with each other, and the contraction and expansion being unequal, most of the ware broke. The firm, however, being very reliable, made good the breakage, and then dropped the line from its list.

For a long period of time Mr. Jaeger has been experimenting with this item, and has successfully developed it, so that it can be placed on the market with absolutely safety. In addition to this new line this firm will also show here a number of new decorations on imported stemware and china.

What can one make of that? The famous peach blow glass of the 1870s being reintroduced in 1927!? Jaeger must have had some access to hot glass, not just a decorating shop, to conduct his "experiments." Recall that Jaeger's earlier venture in Indiana was a complete hot glass factory. What were the facilities in Huntington in this 1920s period? We do not know. We may never know for certain.

The 1930s brought challenge to Bonita. It was re-organized in 1932 as a company, The Bonita Company. Otto Jaeger was yet a stock holder, but no longer the single driving force. *China, Glass and Lamps* in April 1932 noted the "Bonita Glass Corp., glassware decorators of Huntington . . . under the management of W. C. Lerch . . ." It also wrote in September of 1932 that "reports are to the effect that Otto Jaeger, for many years head of Bonita Glass . . . may again take charge of the affairs at the plant." Bonita Glass Corporation had been chartered in 1930. In this circa 1930 period there are some serious financial and corporate shuffles going on at Bonita and the implication is that of hard times. Otto Jaeger died in June of 1941 at age eighty-eight. His story is yet untold and his involvement and innovations only now beginning to be rediscovered.

As late as 1946 and '47 ads appear promoting Bonita Glass. Items shown include blown objects with a pattern imitating crackle glass but with applied leaf decorations on the surface. Examples of ware with Bonita paper labels include real crackle and this blown pattern moulded crackle. This line appears to be distinctive to Bonita. It is an imitation of crackle, blown into a mould with a vein-like pattern resembling crackle glass but without the additional steps in the process. To imitate crackle visually, without the steps necessary to crack and re-fuse the glass, would have been a significant cost-saving measure. Most of the imitation Crackle pieces have applied leaf decorations of glass and are rough pontiled.

The Red Book Directory, a china, glass and giftware buyers index, in 1950 lists "Bonita Glass Co., Huntington, W.Va. J.D. Cober owner and manager . . . blown table-ware, tumblers and stemware, colored glassware, bar and liquor glass ware, novelties and specialties, over the flame ware." Bonita closed in the 1950s.

Bonita Glass Co. All imitation crackle, applied leaf, and rough pontil. Amethyst hat from tumbler form, 2 ¼ inches tall x 5 inches wide at brim, $14-18; green vase with original label, 3 inches, $10-14 without label; aqua tumbler, 6 inches, $12-14.

Bonita Glass Co. Large green crackle glass flip vase with original factory label "Bonita Hand Made", rough pontiled, 8 ¾ inches tall x 5 ¾ diameter, $35-45 without label; small imitation crackle fan vase with applied leaf, rough pontil, $12-15.

Central Glass Works

Central Glass has its origins in one of the Grandfather's of Wheeling Glass: Barnes, Hobbs, & Co. (later Hobbs, Brockunier & Co.). From the Hobbs factory a few disgruntled workers departed to start their own company in 1863. That new upstart company assumed the name Central Glass Co. in 1867.

This large glass house made a great variety of pressed pattern glass until August 1891 when it became a part of the glass combine (monopoly) called U.S. Glass Co. where it was designated as Factory "O". Production ceased shortly after Central joined U.S. Glass and the moulds (thus the patterns) were dispersed to other U.S. Glass Co. factories.

In 1896 local men, including many who had been owners prior to the U.S. Glass takeover, re-purchased the factory. It became Central Glass Works. References in the trade journals seem to fail to always make this distinction and references are inconsistent to the companies name, but advertisements and legal documents consistently call the new firm Central Glass Works. The new owners began to re-establish the production capabilities. This means they had to design and develop, and then have made entirely new moulds for new lines. At the time it may have been burdensome to undertake the task of creating all new ware but by the dawn of the new century taste in glass was changing quickly and new, simpler designs were important to survive.

The company struggled in the early years of the twentieth century. Fire, sales slumps (blamed on inadequate tariff protection), and the death of several of the original investors-enthusiasts were stumbling blocks. In 1899, the *Crockery and Glass Journal* tells that Central had 400 employees. In 1902, the company is reported to have grown to employ nearly 700 people. In 1924, employees numbered 204 men and 44 women. Central would have been a significant force in the glass world throughout this time.

As early as 1901 Central was cited in an unattributed trade journal as producing "the most beautiful line of iridescent stemware the trade has yet seen. All the colors of the rainbow are reflected, yet at first glance one sees only a beautiful clear crystal." As others have observed, this is an early date for iridescent tableware. Yet, Central seems to have been a leader again.

Much of what has been written focuses on Central's pre-merger into U.S. Glass (1893) and, when writing of the post 1896 emergence of Central as an independent company again, we are often told that Central focused on "bar and hotel ware." For most of us that is a instant sign that nothing of interest was happening here. Images of plain, colorless water tumblers and indistinguishable wineglasses flood our minds.

This is inconsistent with what I find reported in trade journals from the 1910s through the 1930s. Glass expert Eason

Eige, writing in *Wheeling Glass: 1829-1939*, quotes a 1936 glass trade journal as saying Central made "high grade tableware, gold decorated and cut stemware and tumblers; etched tableware, hotel and bar glassware." Here is indeed mention of the low end hotel and bar ware. Notice also the lengthier listing of quality glass. This was 1936, *after* the worst of the depression and near the end of Central Glass! Yet production continued to include glass of the type now sought and collected. So exactly what was Central making?

By 1919, Central was able to purchase the moulds for the Chippendale line of pressed pattern glass of Jefferson Glass in nearby Follansbee, West Virginia. In *China, Glass and Lamps* (April 28,1919) we read, " The loss in bar glassware as a result of the country going dry will not affect the Central Glass Works, of Wheeling . . . The business turned over by the Jefferson Glass Co. in Chippendale ware has been so great the company finds itself unable to fill all orders."

This line was long-lived and of great diversity. Indications are it may have been a major success for Central. Patented as early as Feb 5, 1907 by Benjamin W. Jacobs by design patent #38440, this "line" was produced by Jefferson and, prior to that, by an Ohio glass house. It was Central that boomed the pattern. In January 1919 trade journal announcements stated the Chippendale line of over 400 different pieces were being sold by Jefferson Glass of Follansbee, West Virginia, to Central. Jefferson was concentrating on manufacturing lighting goods. The shapes are classic and graceful. Pieces can be found that feature the words Krys-Tol raised in the glass. Occasionally Chippendale and Krys-Tol both appear, as does the patent date. Look in the object's center, look with your fingers first.

An undated catalog, numbered catalog 40, has over twenty pages of just Chippendale pattern. The introduction tells us "The Glass of Quality is so named because it is designed upon the lines of the wonderful Chippendale furniture which although introduced . . . long ago has never been surpassed for beauty or dignity. The characteristic curves of Chippendale [the furniture] have been faithfully reproduced in Chippendale Glass and this together with the purity and brilliance of the glass itself has given Chippendale the remarkable popularity it enjoys in the best homes and among the best classes of people. Chippendale Glass is pure crystal white in color."

A second undated Central Glass Works Chippendale catalog runs on for 55 illustrated pages and includes over 240 then active shapes in the Chippendale line. These range from various sizes of covered cheese dishes to mustard spoons and whip cream bowls with under plates. It is a very extensive line. Not all pieces portrayed have the same stylistic look as Chippendale

To cloud the issue further, while the catalog defines Chippendale as colorless glass, a March 1924 illustrated advertisement of candle sticks and console bowl says "Chippendale Krys-Tol. Console set made in Celeste Blue, Mirror Black, Amethyst, Green Canary and Chinese Jade, also in flat and paste gold encrustations. Central Glass Works". The world of Chippendale pattern glass is wide indeed!

The Frances pattern of pressed glass was another Central success, although never approaching the roaring success of Chippendale. The Frances line appears as a one page addition in the back of a Central catalog copy in the Corning Glass Museum collection. The catalog is dated circa 1931 by Corning. A trade journal ad using the exact same image for the line, calling it only "our line 2010," appeared in 1929. Shown in this vaguely cubist pattern are five variations on a three-toed bowl and one tall vase. The line included tableware and is known to have been produced in rose, green, blue, and amber.

In 1927 Central's display at the Pittsburgh glass show got the following review in *National Glass Budget* (15 Jan 1927): "Central Glass Works [has] a full line of table ware and novelties, decorated and gold encrusted blown stemware. It, also, is showing pressed stemware in colors and Chippendale tableware. This company claims to be the pioneer in manufacturing the popular rose colored glassware, as well as the originators of the salad plates. It is also showing a beautiful line of exquisite shaped, copper wheel engraved high goblets and low English shaped goblets in rock crystal cutting. Its new orchid colored glass presents a beautiful appearance." It appears orchid colored ware by Central was making its first appearance in 1927?

Recent attention, if any, to Central glass of the period between the wars has come to rest on the Harding and Morgan patterns. These are interesting names and stories. Two new plate etchings by Central emerge circa 1920. One is a double pair of griffins, facing one another with additional scrolling, etc., known as deep plate etch 401. This pattern received a design patent June 1, 1920, being design patent no. 55358. The other pattern is a winged sprite or fairy in a circular cameo or swing like circle with heavy floral embellishment, known as deep plate etching 412. This was issued design patent 57570 dated 30 September 1920. The latter at least was the design work of Joseph O. Balda, a free lance designer whose work for Heisey Glass is well respected.

A full page advertisement in *Crockery and Glass Journal* May 26, 1921 shows these two designs and labels them "For America's First Families." The griffin design became the Harding pattern and the sprite became Morgan. A set of 336 pieces in the Harding pattern was given to Mrs. Warren Harding, First Lady, in May of 1921 and used in the White House on state occasions. Being her personal property, she took it with her when the Harding's left the White House. Today parts of the set is preserved in the Harding Presidential Museum in Ohio. (see Spillman, Jane Shadel. *White House Glassware: Two Centuries of Presidential Entertaining*. Washington, D.C.: The White House Historical Association, 1989.) The more fey pattern was given to West Virginia's First Family, the Morgan's, for use in the Governor's Mansion in Charleston, West Virginia. Examples remain there today. Both of these patterns can be found in color-

less, green, blue, amber, in color combinations on stemware, and in Orchid. Complete table settings, pitchers, and serving pieces were produced.

A significant and amazing shape in glass of this early heat resistant glass period is Central's Number 733 Teapot. This colorless glass tea pot appears in an undated circa early 1920s catalog with Deep Plate Etching 10, the thistle design. This leads us to a confusing Central line of this period, Deep Plate Etching 10, Thistle. Like many successful designs in glass, this seems to have been widely adopted. Tiffin Glass and others had their versions of deep plate etched thistle designs. Yet Central's has a striking similarity to a pattern made by Rochester Tumbler Works in Rochester, Pennsylvania. It is made further mysterious when a Central logo appears touting Old Central Quality in a style of type and layout amazingly close to the similar Cooperative Flint Glass Co. (a.k.a. "Coop") of Beaver Fall, Pennsylvania, logo! A question here for future historians is, did Central acquire etching plates, logo, slogan, and other assets of Coop? It would account for amazing similarities, but may be pure conjecture.

I cannot leave Central Glass and their forty plus years after emerging from the U.S. Glass combine as a new and second company without mention of four spectacular objects in the Oglebay Museum Collection, Wheeling, West Virginia. Since first seeing them two decades ago, they have fed my belief that Central was not the neglected and written off producer of "bar and hotel ware."

A interesting gift to Oglebay Mansion Museum in Wheeling, West Virginia, with a family history of having been acquired in the 1930s, includes two elegant 15 inch candle sticks and matching stemmed bowl in blue and opal glass. These are the creation of a highly skilled team of glass crafters. A matching, but not identical, amethyst and opal bowl is also in the Museum collection. These have been regarded suspiciously when attempting to place such pieces into what was thought known of Central's post-1900 production. Today the production by Central is confirmed by a review in *China, Glass and Lamps* dated January 23, 1922 where we read of Central shown at the annual Pittsburgh trade show "the new off-hand ware comes in four colors: amethyst, green, canary and blue. The amethyst and canary are especially worth-while. Some very interesting shapes in bowls, center pieces, and candlesticks are being shown This ware can also be had with a gold decoration. In combinations, the blue has white edging, the amethyst has a white edging and the canary has a black edging. Some of the pieces are also being offered with light cuttings. The center pieces are 10, 12 and 14 inches and come both as high and low-footed. The candlestick shape is very attractive and comes in 10, 12, 15 and 18-inch heights."

Amazing in quality, sheer size, and elegance, these pieces, when found, are often attributed to Steuben or other high end glass producers, yet they come from a company long thought to be producing hotel bar ware at this time!

New stemware introduced in Spring 1930 included a square footed, underside ribbed based design. This line, #1451, appeared with numerous etching on colorless and colored bowls with color combinations for feet and bowl also produced. Green, crystal, and black were the colors employed. At the same time, a line of square tableware came into the line. A long, low, sleek celery, 6, 7, 8, and 9 inch plates, cup and saucer, cream and sugar, a pickle dish, a pastry server with central handle, vegetable dish, grape fruit bowl, and more was available in this pressed line called only 1450. It came in rose, green, and possibly other colors.

In 1931 Central was reported to be showing a "number of new football decorations in their line of decorated highball glasses in their Chicago showroom. The Central highballs can be had in 12 to 16 ounce sizes. Other popular decorations in the Central enamel style are the archery, Scottie dog, and the vari-colored balloon. For the fall college football crowds this Central line should be extremely popular." (CG&L Oct 1931)

Central continued to make hot glass, to introduce new items and to innovate until the very end. *Crockery and Glass* of October 1938 featured, "graceful new cuttings on full lead blanks from Central Glass Co. called Havana, Larieux, and Lenardo."

Central closed late in 1939, declaring bankruptcy. The assets were sold, with a significant amount of the Central property passing to Imperial Glass in nearby Bellaire, Ohio.

Matching candlesticks and console bowl, Central Glass Works. These cobalt and opal/milk glass combination pieces were produced in the elegant art glass style of circa 1922. The candlesticks, 15 inches in height, are comparable to any made in America at that time in design and workmanship. No Price Established. *Collection of Oglebay Institute. Gift of Miss Evelyn M. Forester in memory of Alfred D. and Alice R. Peake.*

Winslow stem, Central Glass Works. Cordial with original factory label on bottom, clear, 3.5 inches, $19-24; cordial, green stem and foot, 3.5 inches, $20-24; wine, cobalt stem and foot, 5 inches, $22-26; cordial, cobalt stem and foot, 3.5 inches, $26-30.

Winslow stem, Central Glass Works. Goblet, Balda plate etching, clear, 6 7/8 inches, $24-28.

A 1937 trade journal ad for Central Glass Works showing "The 1900 Winslow Line."

Thistle plate etching #10, Central Glass Works. Coaster with original factory label, clear, 4 ½ inches. *Courtesy Tom & Neila Bredehoft.* $20-24 without label. Fluted champagne with optic, clear, 6 ½ inches, $18-24.

Central Glass Works catalog pages circa 1930 showing Deep Plate etch #10. This dangling thistle design is strikingly similar to patterns by Tiffin Glass, Rochester Tumbler, and others.

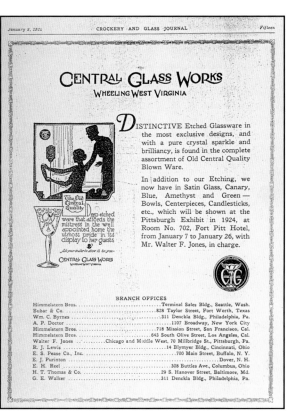

Central Glass Works ad from 1924 includes a Morgan pattern goblet and makes mention of Canary, Blue, Amethyst, and Green, as well as what appears to be a reference to the Bowls and candlesticks in an art glass line shown above. Note: this ad targets "the mistress in the well appointed home."

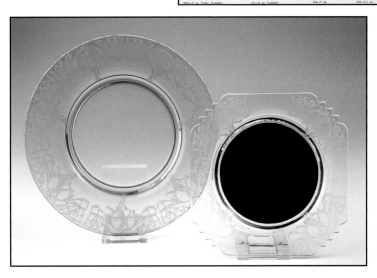

Morgan plate etching, Central Glass Works. Luncheon plate, green, 8 ½ inches, $48-58; dessert plate, Line #1450, clear with reverse painted black plate well, 7 ½ inches, $38-42. Note: Morgan etched dinner plates are scarce, luncheon more common.

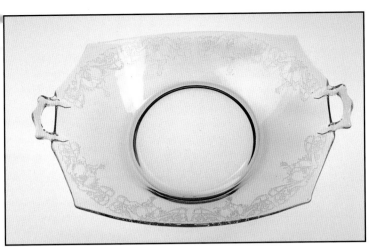

Morgan plate etching, Central Glass Works. Open handled console bowl, 13 2/4 inches, rose, $250-350.

Morgan plate etching, Central Glass Works. Sherbet/saucer champagne, Orchid color, 5 ½ inches, $48-55; sherbet/saucer champagne, clear bowl with green stem and foot, 5 ¾ inches, $65-75.

Morgan plate etching, Central Glass Works. Pink candlesticks, 4 ¾ inches diameter x 3 inches tall, pair $80-100.

Harding plate etching, Central Glass Works. Cup, clear, 2 1/8 inches tall and saucer 5 ¾ inches diameter, $38-48 set; luncheon plate, clear, 8 ½ inches, $25-35.

Pitcher, Harding plate etching #401, Central Glass Works. Pitcher, applied handle, clear, 10 inches, $150-190. Harding was design patent No. 55358, June 1, 1929.

Harding plate etching #401, Central Glass Works. All clear. Low sherbet, 4 ¼ inches, $14-18; low saucer champagne, 5 ¾ inches, $16-18; tall saucer champagne, 6 ¼ inches, $22-28; wine with panel cut stem, 5 ½ inches, $24-26; water goblet, 7 ¾ inches, $28-34.

Harding plate etching, Central Glass Works. Six sided with disk "hokey pokey" or pressed stem cordial, clear, 4 ¼ inches. Same stem as shown later in this chapter, $45-58; grapefruit bowl, clear, 4 ¼ inches tall, $28-34.

Line 1451 stem, Central Glass Works. Harding plate etching #401, square black footed base, clear, optic bowl, 6 inches, $32-38.

Harding plate etching #401, Central Glass Works. Green foot and "old Central spiral" line #1426 stem, clear optic bowl goblet, 7 ½ inches, $40-48; green foot and stem line #1434 tumbler, 5 ¾ inches, $34-38; line #1434 cocktail green foot and stem, clear optic bowl, 3 ¾ inches, $28-36.

"Moderne" stem line #1446, Central Glass Works. Black foot and stem with clear bowl water goblet, 7 ½ inches, $30-36; wine, 5 ½ inches, $28-32. Line shown in ads of 1929.

Blada plate etching, Central Glass Works. All orchid with optic bowls. Footed juice tumbler, 3 inches, $28-38; footed tumbler, 4 ¼ inches, $30-38; footed tumbler, 5 inches, $34-42; saucer champagne, 6 inches, $32-36; saucer champagne, 4 ¾ inches, $32-36; wine, 5 ½ inch, $34-38. The offering in this color-etching combination is extensive and includes serving and other large pieces.

Compote, Central Glass Works. No. 67 tall compote with plate etching #14 form circa 1930 catalog. Optic, clear, 6 ½ inches, $28-34. Wreaths were a popular end of World War I design motif and this etched pattern appears on glass by several companies circa late 1910s.

Stem line #1470, Central Glass Works. Wine with smoke bowl, clear foot and stem, 5 ½ inches, $30-38; cordial, green optic bowl with clear foot and stem, 4 ¾ inches, $40-46.

Harding plate etching, Central Glass Works. Six sided pressed or "hokey pokey" stem with disk, Line #1440 saucer champagne rose, 6 ¼ inches, $60-75.

Central Glass Works. Ruby bowl and clear foot and stem. Same stem, different bowl shape, shown in this chapter with a Morgan etch. 8 inches, $65-80.

Stem line #1470, Central Glass Works. Saucer champagne/sherbet with plate etching and gold encrusted fruit decoration possible by other company, 6 ¼ inches, $25-28; goblet, Hester plate etching #432, topaz or "Golden Saphire" bowl with clear stem and foot, 8 ¼ inches, $45-55. *West Virginia Museum of American Glass collection. Gift of Jeff Conover.*

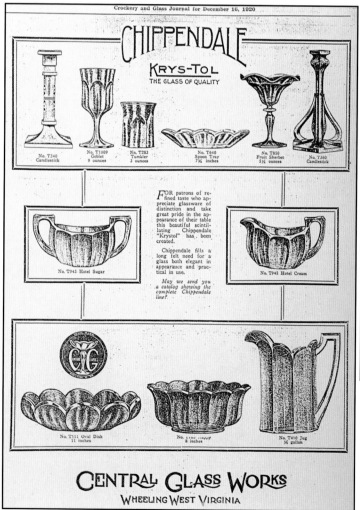

Blada plate etching, Central Glass Works. dessert plate, orchid, 7 ¼ inches, $18-26; amber luncheon plate, 8 ½ inches, $12-16.

A 1920 trade journal ad from *Crockery and Glass Journal* showing the clear pressed pattern Chippendale made in the Krystol line by Central Glass Works. This was a line very like other "colonial," wide panel patterns by Heisey, Imperial, and others at about the same period. Other similarly heavy pressed and thin "elegant" patterns would have also been made simultaneously.

Balda plate etching, Central Glass Works. Rolled edge console bowl, 12 inches diameter x 3 ¼ inches tall, amber, $60-80.

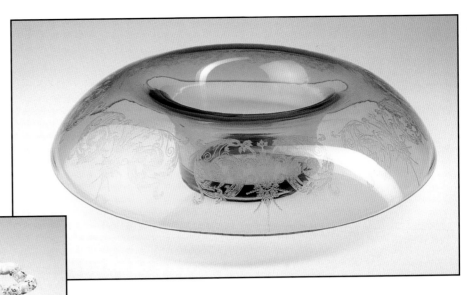

Bowl, Central Glass Works. Small double open handled bowl, plate etching #421 illustrated in circa 1930 catalog. Clear, 7 ½ inches tip of handle to handle. $30-45. *Courtesy Replacements, LTD.*

Balda plate etching, Central Glass Works. Candlestick, 5 inch diameter, 2 ¾ inches tall. Amber Pair: $40-55.

Scott's Morning Glory deep plate etch #5, Central Glass Works. Amber cup, 2 inches tall and saucer 5 1/2 inches diameter, set: $24-32; lilac dessert plate, 7 ½ inches, $18-24.

Scott's Morning Glory deep plate etch #5, Central Glass Works. Cordial, 3 ½ inches, clear, $24-32; orchid footed juice tumbler, $18-20; clear footed water goblet, 5 ¾ inches, $16-20; amber footed and clear optic bowl tumbler, 6 inches, $22-26.

Central Glass Works. Line #1434 orchid optic bowled wine, 3 ¾ inches, $22-28. Line #1440 clear Harding plate etching cordial, 4 inches, $45-58. Line 1440 Balda plate etching saucer champagne, 6 ½ inches, rose, $50-58. These two lines both feature six sided mid-stem disks and can easily be confused.

Variaitons on form and etching, Central Glass Works. The same footed tumbler form with Balada etching on orchid and on green; Scott's Morning Glory etching on orchid. 3 1/3 inches.

Francis pattern, Central Glass Works. Center handled server, green, 10 ¼ inches, $38-48.

Francis pattern, Central Glass Works. Swung vase, 10 ½ inches tall x 9 ½ wide at rim, black, $120-140; swung vase, 8 ¾ inches tall and 8 ½ inches, rose, $60-80.

Francis pattern, Central Glass Works. Two handled celery in vase form, clear, 7 ½ inches, $35-45; four toed celery in low bowl form, clear, 10 ½ inches, $28-38.

Francis pattern, Central Glass Works. Green flared bowl, 9 ½ inches, $35-45; green tri-corn three toed bowl, 9 ½ inches, $48-58.

Francis pattern, Central Glass Works. Moonstone covered powder box with knob finial lid, $75-85; azure blue covered powder box with tab finial lid, $65-80. Both 6 inches.

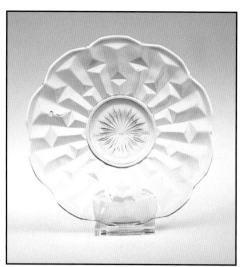

Francis pattern, Central Glass Works. Saucer rose, 6 ¼ inches, $8-12.

Francis pattern, Central Glass Works. Amber creamer, 5 ¼ inches, $28-32; green sugar, 4 ½ inches, $32-36; and green creamer, 5 ¼ inches, $32-36.

Greek plate etching #7, Central Glass Works. Goblet, clear, 6 ½ inches, $32-36; wine, 4 inches, $20-26; straight sided tumbler, 5 inches, $18-22; sherbet, 3 inches, $16-22; plate with metal filigree border, 6 ¼ inches, $22-26; plate with metal filigree border, 7 ¼ inches, $ 24-28.

Goblet, Central Glass Works. Optic bowl etch #14, clear, 6 ½ inches, $20-26. *West Virginia Museum of American Glass collection.*

Line #1451 square base, Central Glass Works. Footed tumbler, clear base with rose bowl, 5 ½ inches, $14-18; footed tumbler, clear base and amber with unknown etching (possibly decorated by another company), 4 inches, $20-24; footed tumbler, black base and green optic bowl, 5 ¾ inches, $24-28.

Central Glass Works. Footed bowl amber with loop optic, 7 ½ inches, $28-32. *West Virginia Museum of American Glass collection.*

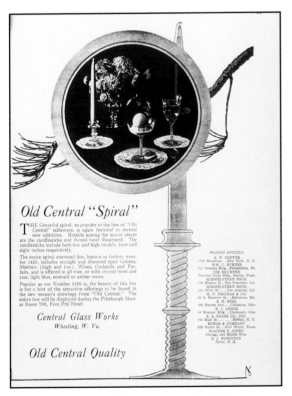

Central Glass Works letterhead dated 1922 proclaiming they are at that time manufacturing the Chippendale pattern, Krys-Tol line, and "The Old Central Quality Ware."

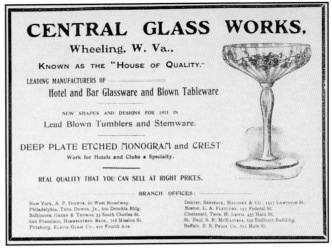

This circa 1920s trade journal ad shows Central Glass Works deep plate etching #6, a grape pattern. Grape etched patterns by various glass companies are strikingly similar and easily confused.

"Old Central Spiral" stem Line #1426, Central Glass Works. Saucer champagne/sherbet, rose stem and foot with clear optic bowl, 4 ¾ inches, $16-22; saucer champagne/sherbet, all rose with optic bowl, 5 ½ inches, $18-22.

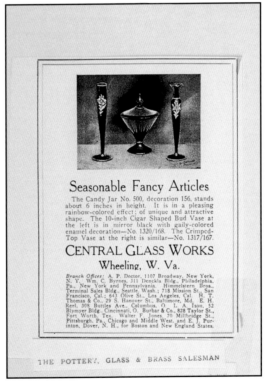

Central Glass Works full page ad appearing in *The Pottery, Glass & Brass Salesman* of December 1925 shows the Old Central Spiral line, "factory number 1426," which it claims as popular, was then adding new items. Shown are a candlestick, sherbet, and goblet.

This illustrated ad from *Pottery, Glass and Brass Salesman* in 1925 includes black glass, "rainbow-colored" or iridescent glass, and enamel decorations. All of these were popular glass treatments for the time.

"Old Central Spiral" Line #1426, Central Glass Works. Hokey pokey stem, rose with diamond optic bowl, 7 ½ inches, $22-32. *West Virginia Museum of American Glass collection.*

Black amethyst Line #1450, Central Glass Works. Luncheon set cup and saucer, $24-28; dessert plate, 7 ½ inches, $12-16; luncheon plate, 8 ½ inches, $14-18. Enamel decorated peacock on black amethyst "cigar shaped" bud vase (as per the previous ad copy), this example with original factory label on bottom, 10 inches, $45-55 without label.

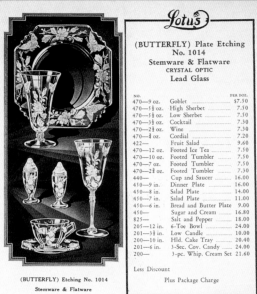

This department store pamphlet promotes The Butterfly etching by Lotus Glass of Ohio. However the step cornered Central lines #1459 tableware and stemware line #1470 are all products of Central Glass with decorations by Lotus. Lotus was a major consumer of Central Glass in the 1920 and '30s.

Plate etching #408, Central Glass Works. Azure blue bowl clear stem, goblet, 7 ¼ inches, $40-45; saucer champagne, 5 ½ inches, $30-40; salad plate, azure blue, 7 ½ inches, $18-24.

Columbia Glass Co.

This little known factory in Fairmont, West Virginia, made a variety of products—a few of which were glass staples, well known in the time between the world wars. Columbia Glass Company began in 1907 and operated under that name until 1932. From 1932 until 1961 it operated as Commercial Glass Co. In 1940, it was listed in the *American Glass Review Yearbook* as Commercial Glass with one continuous tank and two day tanks for production.

A catalogue illustrates ointment and salve jars in milk or opal glass. Included are the hand blown, lifelike eggs used to "trick" hens to stay on their nests and lay, called nesting eggs. It is likely these two lines were major production items for Columbia.

The company also made hand painted Easter eggs in many sizes and patterned salt and pepper shakers. It should be noted that all of these products were made in opal (milk) glass only. The hand painted Easter eggs are highly collectable, and were a popular part of Easter baskets for several decades. White opaque glass may have been the only type of glass made by Columbia. The catalogue text refers to "beautifully shaded in pink, blue, green and yellow with flowers painted on it to match the shaded tint," suggesting the colors were painted, or "tinted" on opal glass, the color not being in the glass itself. Further in the catalogue, a 10 ½ inch "colonial shape" vase is illustrated with hand painting. It is designated Vase No. 8, so it is quite possible there are opal glass hand painted vases in other sizes.

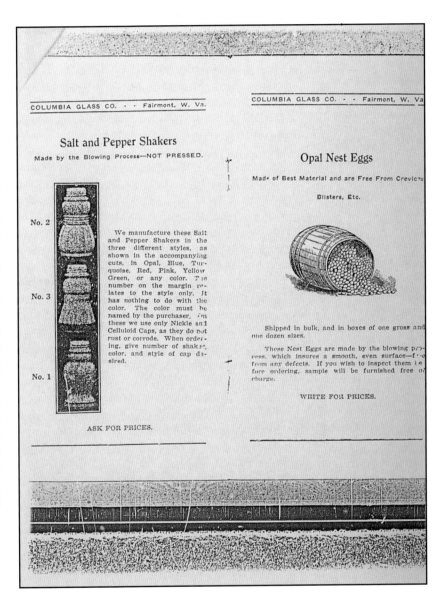

This two page spread from an undated Columbia Glass catalog dates to the 1920s and includes the type of "opal" or milk glass the company thrived on.

Dunbar Glass

For almost thirty years, centered in the period this book focuses on, Dunbar Glass was a large and significant glass producer. The corporate names changed a few times over the years as financial restructuring occurred, but it remained on the same site with the same basic owners. On 6 July 1923 Dunbar Flint Glass Corporation was chartered. They purchased the existing glass factory of the Pennsylvania Glass Co., a bottle manufacturer, in Dunbar, West Virginia. Dunbar Flint Glass began its life as a producer of lamp chimneys, a major product in its day of pre-electricity.

Dunbar began to press glass in 1927 and remained a large producer for years. Yet how seldom does glass appear on the collector's market identified as Dunbar? *The National Glass Budget* 15 January 1927, telling of the Pittsburgh glass show, states "on the tables and shelves of the Dunbar Flint Glass Corporation . . . may be seen pressed tumblers, vases, marmalades, tableware, etc. There are also blanks for cutting, lamp chimneys, and a complete line of colored, decorated and cut glass. One of their special offerings is the 19 piece beverage set that sells for one dollar." Apparently their tableware lines were popular. An ad in *China, Glass & Lamps* of 24 December 1928 states "3,500 beverage sets sold in One Day was the record of one Chicago store". The line featured iced tea sets, covered pitchers with glasses. And, we are told, ". . . for 1929 Dunbar offers their entire line of popular priced glassware in the choice of two colors. A new shade of green and an attractive shade of rose pink".

In 1930, as the depression hit hardest, Dunbar laid off no employees, but slowed production. Their capacity at the time was three continuous tanks and two day tanks for a total of nine rings. If you don't speak glass production, let me assure you that translates into immense production capacities.

We are fortunate in that a catalogue introducing the Dunbar line for 1931 has survived. In the roughly sixty pages an amazing variety of ware is shown. Today collector's would call this "elegant Depression Glass." Colors include Rose Pink, Bermuda Green, and black glass. With classic and modern design, tableware, and endless other shapes, it is amazing Dunbar glass has gone so unnoticed by collectors.

In 1932, Dunbar launched a national promotion featuring the designs of John Held, Jr. Prohibition was no more. Dunbar appeared in *The New Yorker* and *Vogue* and other up scale publications. It was sold in Macy's and Bloomingdale's.

When metal became a scarce commodity in World War II, the role of glass changed quickly and dramatically. One of my favorite quotes in this regard comes from the April 1943 issue of the *West Virginia Review*, "Contrary to the belief of the average person, the plastics industry has been a great friend to the glass industry in that glass parts may now be used in a great many places in conjunction with plastic parts, whereas, prior to the advent of modern plastics, glass parts frequently could not be used because of mechanical limitations. An example of this is the use of cooking utensil accessory parts made of plastic which has made possible the growing trend in glass cooking utensils. Mrs. America now seems thoroughly pleased with the idea. She has learned that heat-resistant glassware has a reasonably long life when cared for properly. It has the advantage of visibility, enabling the housewife to see at a glance how her cooking is progressing. It is easily cleaned and certainly highly decorative in modern kitchens. All indications are that the market for glass ware, boosted by the war, will not be merely a duration product, but one that will become increasingly popular in American homes."

And right this prophecy was. However, Dunbar was not to win the glass cookware battle, other larger companies did. For the years during and shortly after World War II Dunbar prospered. In 1943 the factory covered several acres.

During this early 1940s time a spokesperson appears for Dunbar Glass. This lady is Jane Dunbar, a competitor for Betty Crocker and an early marketing tool. Seemingly entirely fictional, Jane Dunbar is found in *The Saturday Evening Post*, *Ladies' Home Journal*, and *Crockery & Glass Journal*, to name a few, from 1944 to 1946 and perhaps beyond. Her suggestions "for smart kitchen ware" and that "glass brightens kitchens, lightens cooking chores" all promoted Dunbar's colorless glass cookware in a time of war time metal rationing.

The ultimate Jane Dunbar promotion is a sixteen page booklet with a title *Glamour in Glass* by Jane Dunbar (!) featuring a dramatic sketch of light passing through a cathedral window. Inside, a brief history of glass places heat resistant Dunbar in a long context of glass evolution. Illustrations include a "black and white and crystal kitchen," in the up to date monochrome scheme! And there are slogans: "Dunbar cooking glass is moderately priced," "It's a kitchen jewel," and "strong flavors do not cling to glass like they do to many other materials," plus several others.

In the 1930s and probably into the 1940s Dunbar produced an endless array of "mirror finished" glass. This was a line of thin, paste mould, hand formed, mouth blown usually colorless glass with a light irridescent or "mirror" finish. Pitcher and tumbler sets are found as well as a great variety of vases made to fit into metal frames. Many of these pieces were made in identical shapes, with and without bases. Those that lack feet or the ability to stand alone require a footed or wall mounting, usually black, metal support.

Dunbar pitcher and tumbler sets can be found in a transparent green, cobalt blue and ruby red, often in the same shapes as the mirror finished sets.

In 1949, *China & Glass* said Dunbar had a "substantial business in blown and pressed glassware for lighting fixtures use, special private mold glassware, heat resistant cooking glassware, and a full line of vases and bowls of particular interest to the florist trade." As late as the early 1950s, Dunbar is quoted as having 1,200 employees!

World War Two caused a great boom for Dunbar Glass as it did for many other American industries. As the expansion of the war years faded Dunbar struggled to identify the correct product line that would remain profitable. In 1953 the board of directors announced that they "decided to withdraw from the blown and pressed glass business and concentrate on the machine drawn tubing development which the firm embarked on several months ago." Shortly thereafter Dunbar closed forever.

Dunbar Glass. Rings tumbler, cobalt blue, 5 inch, $14-20; jug, pink ringed with applied handle, 7 inches, $68-78. *West Virginia Museum of American Glass collection.*

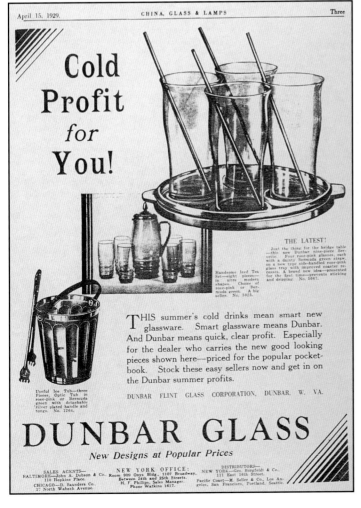

Jugs, Dunbar Glass. Tall ringed light blue, $60-80; and clear with iridescence luster, $40-55; both 10 inches. Known in cobalt blue.

Dunbar ad from 1929 features tumblers, tray, and glass drinking straws for "the bridge table," iced tea or ice bucket, all available in Bermuda green or rose pink.

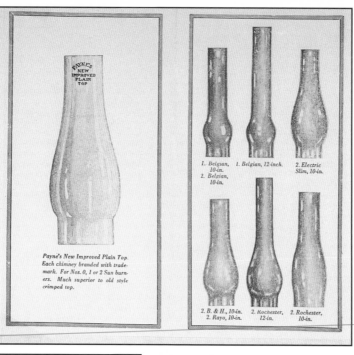

BEST SELLERS
IN
Lamp Chimneys

SAVE MONEY
*Buy Direct from the Factory
or Our Nearest Warehouse*

DUNBAR-FLINT GLASS CORP.
DUNBAR, WEST VIRGINIA

*Payne's New Improved Plain Top.
Each chimney branded with trademark. For Nos. 0, 1 or 2 Sun burn-
ers. Much superior to old style
crimped top.*

1. Belgian, 10-in.
2. Belgian, 10-in.
1. Belgian, 12-inch.
2. Electric Slim, 10-in.

2. B. & H., 10-in.
2. Rayo, 10-in.
2. Rochester, 12-in.
2. Rochester, 10-in.

One side of a pamphlet featuring what was a main source of income for Dunbar and many other glass houses, lamp chimneys. In rural America oil lamps continued to provide light well into the 1940s.

When American went to war, metals were rare commodities. Kitchen glass received a major boom in this era. This 1945 Dunbar ad from the immensely popular *Saturday Evening Post* is a strong testimonial to the success of war time "smart cooking glass."

Vase, Dunbar Glass Corp. Twist optic with hand painted decoration, pink, 8 inches, $12-18 as shown.

DUNBAR GLASS CORPORATION   DUNBAR, WEST VIRGINIA

1138-L

5130

1160-1219

3032

5210

5205

5216

3020

Original catalog page, Dunbar 1931 catalog. Items available in rose pink or Bermuda green. Note the appearance of the glass straws shown in the ad above.

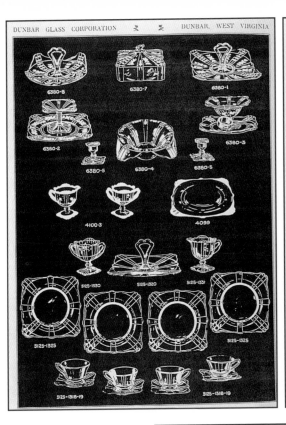

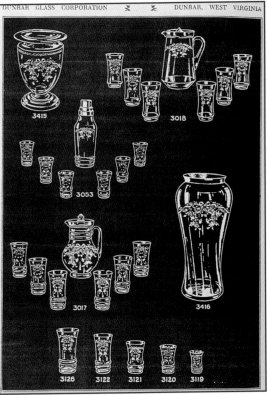

Left: Original catalog page, Dunbar 1931 catalog. Items available in rose pink or Bermuda green. Note this is the only tableware line shown in the 1931 Dunbar catalog. Oddly luncheon plates, cups, etc. are line #5125 and accessories such as candlesticks, candy boxes, and center handled servers are line #6380. Both lines appear identical in design.

Right: Original catalog page, Dunbar 1931 catalog. Items available in rose pink or Bermuda green. The decoration shown is noteworthy from Dunbar.

Center handled server, Dunbar Glass Corp. Bermuda green, 10 inches diameter, $25-34. Part of an extensive tableware pattern that includes cream, sugar, plates, etc. shown in the 1931 catalog. *West Virginia Museum of American Glass collection.*

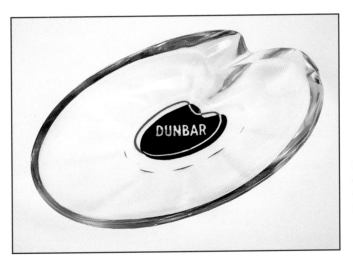

Dunbar Glass Corp. Ash tray, colorless with red and black enamel decoration. Ash tray, when with cigarette in cigarette rest, resembles Dunbar corporate logo of artists palette and brush. 6 inches, $45-55.

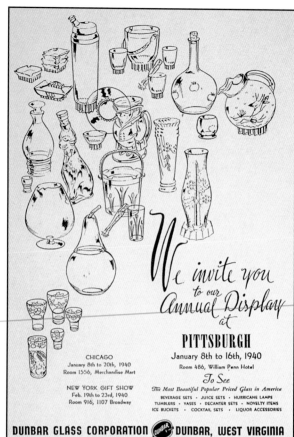
Left: Dunbar ad December 1928 from *China, Glass & Lamps* reports 3,500 beverage sets sold in *One Day*. The top right, #5024 jug was long in production and appears to have been one of the best Dunbar sellers. It appears elsewhere in illustrations in this chapter.

Right: This trade journal ad for the 1940 Pittsburgh trade show features an amazing insight into Dunbar shapes and products on the eve of the Second World War. The Toby mug was continued in production well into the 1980s by Dunbar's successor, Kanawha Glass.

Dunbar was stretching in this 1937 *China, Glass & Lamps* trade journal ad where jugs and tumblers include "sand blast," "Lustre Colors," hand cutting, and gold banding as decorations.

Cookie Jar, Dunbar Glass Corp. Jar with rings and gray hand cutting. Pressed lid with distinctive open triangle finial. Pink. 1931 Dunbar catalog # 6441-3. 6 1/8 inches to top of jar, $40-50.

Dunbar Glass Corp. Ringed shapes crafted from the same mold. Jug/pitcher, lustered amber body and blue handle, $30-40; clear two handled clear urn vase, $25-35 (shown damaged, priced in good condition); pitcher, clear body with green painted handle, $25-35. All 9 ½ inches.

Rings tumblers, Dunbar Glass Corp. Twist optic tumblers #1158 shown in 1931 catalog. Here with black band decoration and coaching scene decal retouched by hand with paint, note color variances, pink, 4 1/8 inches, $12-18 each.

Left: This "smart" 1937 Dunbar ad shows ultramodern form and sand blast decoration on colorless glass.

Right: Dunbar offerings for Christmas 1928 included "rose and pink" as well as gold encrusted Rambler Rose designs, commonly attributed to Tiffin and others, "gold inlaid design the latest in art treatment in glassware." *China, Glass & Lamps* October 1928.

Satin decorated vase, Dunbar Glass Corp. Ringed vase with optic, clear with satin finish and gold banding, 10 inches, $22-28.

Ringed jug No. 5024, Dunbar Glass Corp. Rose pink body with applied green handle and green pressed lid, 9 ¾ inches to top of jug pink, $80-95.

Jug with lid, Dunbar Glass Corp. Melon form # 1135 with hand applied handle and pressed lid. Pink. Note the distinctive finial. Shown in 1931 Dunbar catalog. 9 ½ inches to top of jug, $65-80.

This illustrated Dunbar ad from the late 1920s was featured in the *Annual China and Glass Directory*. It highlights the popular No. 5024 jug or "Iced Tea Set."

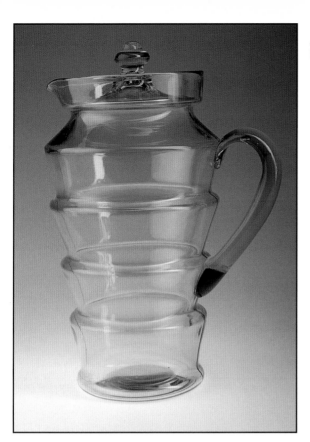

Jug with lid, Dunbar Glass Corp. Diminishing rings form with applied handle and pressed lid. Pink. Note the distinctive finial. 9 ½ inches to top of jug, $65-80.

Dunbar Glass Corp. #1112-5 tumbler, pink, 4 ½ inches, $6-10; pitcher with applied handle, 7 ½ inches, $45-55.

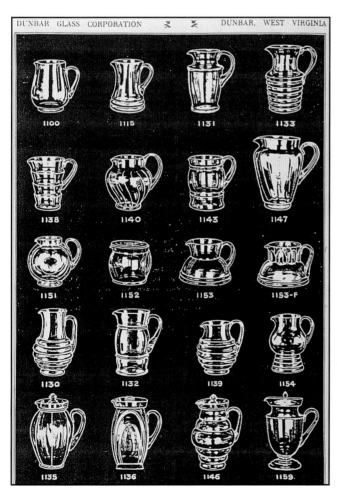

Original catalog page, Dunbar 1931 catalog. Items available in rose pink or Bermuda green.

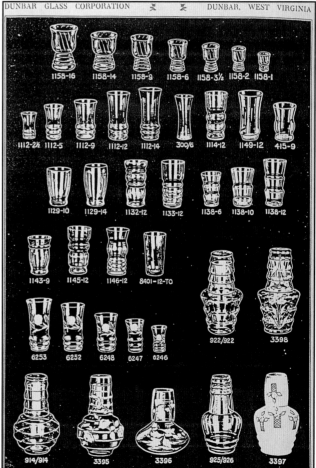

Original catalog page, Dunbar 1931 catalog. Items available in rose pink or Bermuda green. Selection of tumbler up sets included with decorations.

Two-tone iridescent luster, Dunbar Glass Corp. Crimped top into jack-in-the-pulpit form created from tumbler molds. Blue to rose iridescent luster, 4 ½ inches, $18-22; 5 ¼ inches, $20-26; and 2 ½ inches, $18-24.

Footed tumblers, Dunbar Glass Corp. Footed sherbets, diminishing rings, amber/topaz luster and blue luster, 3 inches, $12-16 each.

Tumble Up or night bottle, Dunbar Glass Corp. Water bottle without tumbler-lid, Bermuda Green, 9 1/4 inches as shown. $25-30 without lid.

Ringed jug, Dunbar Glass Corp. Applied handle and blue iridescent luster or "mirror finish," 9 ¾ inches, $25-35.

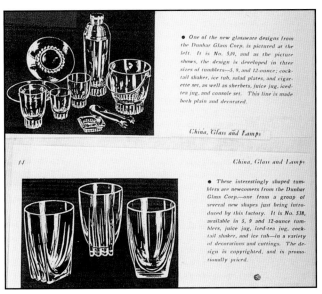

Circa 1940 trade journal announcements of Dunbar lines as they appeared in *China, Glass and Lamps*.

Acorn form vases, Dunbar Glass Corp. Footed with light luster, 6 ½ inches, $12-18; green luster in white metal frame, 14 ½ inches to top of frame, $14-20.

Rings shape, Dunbar Glass Corp. Bermuda green pitcher with ice lip and applied handle, 9 ¾ inches, $55-65; tumbler, 5 inches, $9-14; 3 ¾ inches, $8-12.

Rings tumblers, Dunbar Glass Corp. Iridescent luster blue, green pink, orange/marigold. All 4 inches, $8-12 each.

Rings tumblers, Dunbar Glass Corp. Bermuda green, $12-18; pink luster, $10-14; both 4 ¾ inches; blue and amber luster, 5 ½ inches, $12-18.

"12 inch optic vase No. 4072" from the 1928 ad previously shown, Dunbar Glass. Thin blown vase, pink with partial Dunbar label. Museum purchase, closed Cincinnati, Ohio, iron works firm. 11 ½ inches. *West Virginia Museum of American Glass* collection. $20-26 without label.

Holiday Glassware from Dunbar as shown in *China, Glass & Lamps* October 1928. Note the No. 4077 "Checo Vase" and 12 inch optic vase No.4072, both of which appear at left.

Ringed No.4077 "Checo" Vase, Dunbar Glass Corp. Ruby luster body, clear at rim with gray hand cutting. Luster in the manner popularized in the 1940s, note darker than earlier colors. 6 ½ inches tall, 6 inches wide, $18-24.

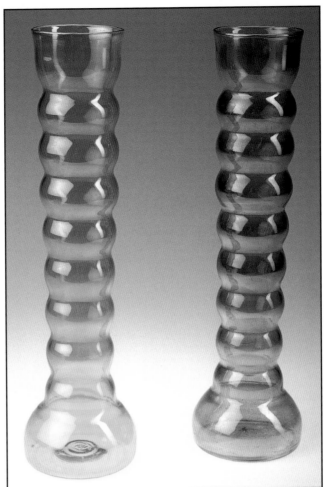

Rings Vase, Dunbar Glass Corp. Tall bulging rings bud vase, green iridescence luster, $12-18; and marigold/orange iridescent luster, $12-18; both 9 inches.

Vase, Dunbar Glass Corp. Colorless iridescent luster, ground top, clear. Florist vase, 7 ¾ inches tall, 3 ½ x 7 inches at top. Form identical to that also created in pottery. $22-28.

Dunbar Glass ringed, blue luster vase for use in metal stand, 6 ¾ inches, $20-24 with stand; glass vase in metal holder marigold/orange iridescent glass, 10 inches, $20-26; acorn form vase for use in metal stand, marigold/orange optic and iridescent luster with original Dunbar factory label, 5 inches, $20-28 with stand and without label.

Close-up of Dunbar Glass paper label from acorn vase shown. Museum purchase, from closed Cincinnati, Ohio, metal working firm factory. *West Virginia Museum of American Glass* collection.

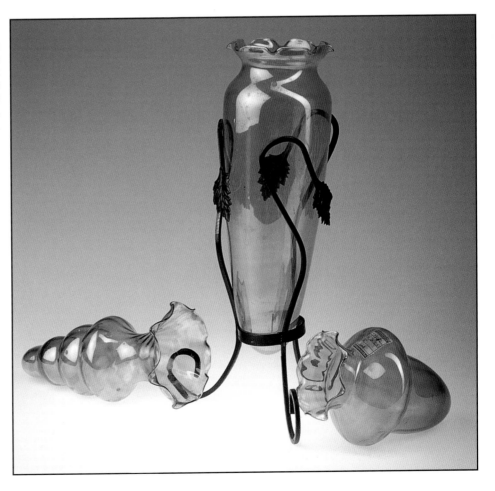

Fenton Art Glass

Fenton Art Glass Co. began operations in Williamstown, West Virginia, in 1907. Today it continues to produce quality glass. During the period between the world wars Fenton production included glass that today is collected as "elegant depression." It included hand made, light colored tableware, vases, candy dishes, etc. Later in the period of our interest Fenton adopts Victorian pattern glass forms and makes a great deal of glass in the style of an earlier time. Fenton is significant to the story of West Virginia Glass for many reasons. It remains active when all of its major competitors have ceased to exist. It has provided leadership for the glass industry, within the state and nation. And, like Hobbs Glass a century before, many of the key players in American and West Virginia glass have had some relationship with Fenton at one time or another.

The West Virginia glass story would be incomplete without tribute to this glass success story. It would be unwise to try to tell the Fenton story that has been told by several authors, in varying ways, and quite well. For Fenton I will allow some of the "between the wars" product to do the talking. Let me suggest the following books on Fenton for further information.

Heacock, William. *Fenton Glass: The First Twenty-Five Years.*
    Marietta, Ohio: O-Val Advertising Corp., 1978. 144 p.
Heacock, William. *Fenton Glass: The Second Twenty-Five Years.*
    Marietta, Ohio: O-Val Advertising Corp., 1980. 154 p.

Lincoln Inn pattern #1700, Fenton Art Glass Co. Footed tumbler, 7 oz., jade green, 4 inches, $26-30; sherbet, jade green, 4 ¼ inches, $20-26; sherbet, clear, 4 ¼ inches, $6-10; cup, amethyst/"orchid" (less common color), 2 ½ inches, $16-18. Produced 1928-late 1930s.

Threaded Mosaic vase, Fenton Art Glass Co. Off hand #3051 cobalt foot and open handles, 1925 only, 11 inches tall, $750-850.

Threaded Mosaic vase, Fenton Art Glass Co.
Threaded mosaic #3007 vase, 9 ½ inches, 1925
only, $540-640. Roy and Doris White collection.

Lincoln Inn Line full page
advertisement run by
Fenton Art Glass in *China,
Glass & Lamps* in
December 1928.

Lincoln Inn as featured in a Butler Bros.
wholesale catalog of the 1930s. No mention
of the manufacturer is made. The pieces
shown are with the fruit center, commonly
found on larger objects.

Cornucopia candleholders, 5 ¾ inches, Fenton Art Glass Co. #950, Mandarin red, $48-58 each; and amber, $20-30 each.

Fenton Art Glass was offered in an opalescent assortment of twelve shapes in this Butler Bros. wholesale catalog illustration from circa 1940.

Fenton Art Glass Co. Floral cigarette box with lid clear with frosted floral– shown with lid on, $35-45; Mongolian green cigarette box with design on underside of lid shown with lid off, circa 1934-35, $90-120. Both 4 ½ inches x 3 ½ inches.

Historic American pattern, Fenton Art Glass Co. Cup plate, Mount Vernon, clear, 4 inches, no value given (Heacckock noted this difficult to find); Niagara Falls luncheon plate, clear, 7 ¾ inches, $35-45. Other pieces in the line have other views. Reported as made circa 1937 as exclusive for Macy's and affiliates.

Fenton Art Glass Co. Shapes from mold #847. Mongolian green melon form bowls flared out, 5 inches tall, 10 inches in diameter, $45-55; abstract cupped form, 5 ½ inches tall, 6 inches diameter at widest point, $35-45. Both circa mid-1930s.

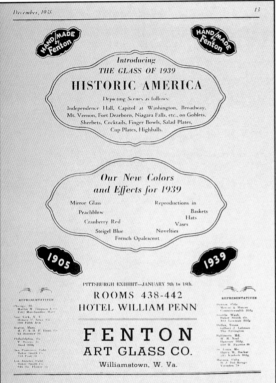

This full page ad in *China, Glass & Lamps* of December 1938 offered the pattern Historic America to the world, it no longer being a Macy's exclusive. Note also the new colors and effects for 1939.

Tumbler, Fenton Art Glass Co. Diamond optic footed tumbler #1641-1702, Ruby, circa 1928, 11 oz., 5 ¼ inches, $18-24.

Baskets, Fenton Art Glass Co. Baskets #1681 with wicker handle, Madarin red, Big Cookies basket, 10 ½ inches, $130-150; jade green #1684 basket, 9 inches, $150-170; banded pattern mandarin basket, 4 inches, #1684, $90-100. *Roy and Doris White collection.*

Console bowl, Fenton Art Glass Co. Oval console bowl #1633, clear with frosted panels, clear, 13 inches, $20-28. Circa 1920-30s.

A 1932 trade journal ad for Fenton Art Glass announcing "something really new" – vases and bowls with pedestals. Colors cited in the ad include Pekin Blue, Chinese yellow, Moonstone, or Jade. They were promoted as "an especially attractive radio set."

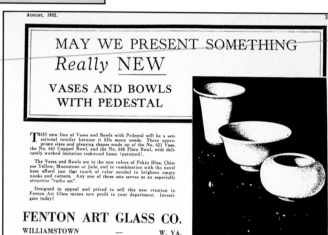

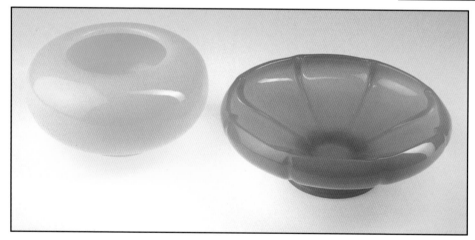

Fenton Art Glass Co. Chinese yellow #846 cupped bowl, 6 ¼ inches, circa 1932, $28-38; jade green melon bowl #847, cupped, 7 ½ inches diameter, $35-45. Both 1930s.

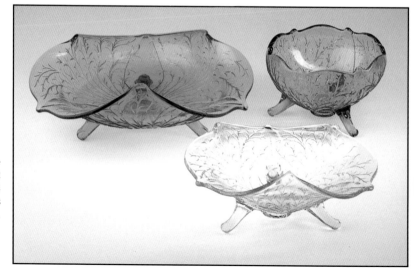

Silverton pattern, Fenton Art Glass Co. Three toed bowls. Tri-crimped "club shaped" #1001 amber, 9 ¼ inches at widest point, $18-22; "club shaped" #1006 aquamarine blue, 6 ¼ at widest point, $20-24; cupped amber #1007, 5 inches diameter, $13-15. Produced 1934-1938.

Fenton Art Glass Co. Mandarin red bowl, 8 ½ inches diameter, #846, $50-65; vase #621, 6 inches, $50-56; low cupped bowl, 2 ½ inches x 8 ½ inches diameter, $45-55; lobed fan vase, 5 ½ inches, $50-55. Production 1924-1935. *Roy and Doris White collection.*

Fenton Art Glass Co. Mandarin red #888 ribbed vase, 10 inches, $250-280.

A 1937 *China, Glass & Lamps* ad for Fenton Art Glass promoted the Wistaria decoration on clear glass.

CG&L MAR 37

Fostoria

Fostoria Glass Co. was organized in Wheeling, West Virginia, in 1887 and later that same year produced its first glass in a Fostoria, Ohio, factory. However, the West Virginia connections ran deep and when natural gas availability became an issue at the end of 1891 the company relocated to Moundsville, West Virginia, a few short miles below Wheeling on the Ohio River.

Fostoria reigned as a (some would insist "the") dominant quality American tableware manufacturer by the end of World War II. The company closed in 1986 although the name is yet used to market glass production from glass houses around the world by present "Fostoria" owner, Lancaster Colony Corp.

The Fostoria story, like Fenton's, is told in a number of good books. Shown here is a snippet of the between the wars Fostoria. Several books deal with just parts of the production that spanned over a century. Suggested reading includes:

Kerr, Ann. *FOSTORIA: An Identification and Value Guide of Pressed, Blown and Hand Molded Shapes.* Paducah, Kentucky: Collector Books, 1994. 230 p.

Long, Milbra and Emily Seate. *Fostoria Stemware: The Crystal for America.* Paducah, Kentucky: Collector Books, 1995.

Long, Milbra and Emily Seate. *Fostoria Tableware 1924-1943: The Crystal For America.* Paducah, Kentucky: Collector Books, 1999. 336 p.

Piña, Leslie. *FOSTORIA: Serving the American Table 1887-1986.* Atglen, Pennsylvania: Schiffer Publishing Co., 1995. 197 p.

Victorian pattern, Fostoria Glass Co. Single candlestick, clear foot, amethyst/"burgundy" body, 6 inches, 1933-38, $40-56; goblet, clear foot and stem, green bowl, 6 inches, 1933-42, $30-36; sherbet/saucer champagne, 4 ½ inches, $28-31.

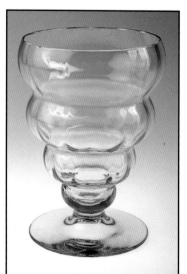

Line 4101, Fostoria Glass Co. Azure blue bubble footed tumbler, circa 1920s, 4 ¾ inches, $20-24.

Fostoria ad appearing in *Good Housekeeping* December 1930. Elegant nut cups and ebony smoking accessories make this ad appeal to an urban consumer as the great depression takes hold of America.

By 1938 Fostoria was seeking to help Americans move beyond the depression. The "modern" beverage set was made in amber, Regal blue, azure blue, and crystal.

■ The beverage set at the left is one of three new designs brought out for this season by the Fostoria Glass Co. It is made in amber, Regal blue, azure blue, and crystal, and is available with two sizes of tumblers—12-ounce, as pictured here, or 10-ounce. The seven-piece set with 12-ounce tumblers can be retailed for $3.50; with 10-ounce tumblers, for $3.25.

April, 1938

[ADV.]

Candlestick #2372, Fostoria Glass Co. Mushroom form grape etching "Brocade etching #287," green, 1927-1929, 1 ½ inches tall x 4 inches diameter, $55-65 pair.

June plate etching #279, Fostoria Glass Co. Line #5098 with June plate etching, 1928-1940. Clear foot and pink bowl footed tumbler, 5 inches, $20-24; and saucer champagne/sherbet, 6 inches, 28-32. Another of the highly popular Fostoria patterns.

4020 line, Fostoria Glass Co. Square base green foot and stem sherbet or saucer champagne, 4 ½ inches, $15-20; goblet, 5 ¾ inches, $20-25; sherbet or saucer champagne, clear foot and stem, topaz bowl with plate etching #284 "New Garden," circa 1930-33, $20-26; goblet, black foot and stem with clear bowl, 5 ¾ inches, $18-24.

Fostoria American clear oval platter, 12 inches, $55-65; tumbler, 3 ½ inches, $12-14; tumbler, 4 inches, $13-16. Perhaps the most produced pattern in American pressed glass!

Footed tumbler blank #4020, Fostoria Glass Co. Green foot, clear bowl, plate etching #285 Minuet. 4 inches, $30-33.

Versialles plate etching #278, Fostoria Glass Co. All rose #4100, 1928-1934, vase, 8 inches, $130-150; creamer, 3 ½ inches, $30-36; ice bucket with metal handle, 1929-1932, 6 inch to top of glass, $120-140. Versailles was very popular then and today. *Courtesy Replacements, LTD.*

The bold Fostoria design of Flame, Nocturne, and Baroque lines as illustrated in *Woman's Home Companion* December 1936. Noted was the "new" azure crystal, a light blue.

Silver Mist

★

with all the haunting beauty of rare old "Camphor Glass"

Here is another important "revival"...Silver Mist...Fostoria's latest triumph in glass-making technique. Here is glassware almost too beautiful to describe...glassware you might have looked for in the prized collection of a connoisseur, but which you would certainly not have expected to find in today's stores, priced well within your reach.

When you see it, we believe you will agree that we have retained in Silver Mist all the satin sheen of fine old "Camphor Glass". Perhaps you will feel, as we do, that our reproduction is an improvement on the original. Write for our booklet on Correct Wine and Table Service. Fostoria Glass Company, Moundsville, W. Va.

. . . . .

The pieces illustrated are:—footed fruit bowl and candlesticks to match, "Trindle", decanter, flower vase, candy jar, bitters bottle, three-part relish dish and the popular Fostoria "Bubble Ball". These are just a few of the beautiful Fostoria pieces in "Silver Mist".

Fostoria — THE GLASS OF FASHION

Silver Mist was promoted in May 1934 as Fostoria's revival of "rare old camphor glass." It was a satin finished crystal treatment on several lines and shapes. Note the candlesticks in the foreground are shown above in color.

This 1920s Fostoria ad shows heavier, clear pressed glass with decoration. These are types of glass not commonly recognized as Fostoria.

Fostoria

FINE CRYSTAL AND DECORATED GLASSWARE

You have been in homes where each room is a little stage with a perfect setting. Every table, every mirror, every candlestick "belongs" absolutely. . . . You remember high lights. Perhaps a shining crystal bowl that reflected the glory of the open fire. Or the swift dazzle of glass at the table laid for formal dinner. . . . Is there a corner that's out-of-keeping in your house? A whole room that's lifeless because it lacks color? Fostoria brings out lights and shadows; it belongs. . . . From the fragile iridescent bubbles of goblets to the rich gold-encrusted treasure-pieces, Fostoria is accepted by women whose taste is perfection. It is sold in the finest shops. Fostoria specializes in glassware service. You may have worried about what glass to use. Send today for "A Little Book About Glassware," which describes the etiquette of the glassware service and the art of using fine crystal. Address The Fostoria Glass Company, Moundsville, W. Va.

Shining crystal striped with silver mist

A STRIKING use of satin-like etching gives this pleasing variation of the popular Sun-Ray pattern a lively character. Glacier stands out against any background as charming and practical crystalware.

Fostoria craftsmen have put the Glacier design on over 80 different pieces...complete sets including plates of many sizes, tumblers, bowls, and incidental dishes. Here are delightful gifts, both for those who get them and those who give them.

Your dealer is displaying this beautiful new pattern and at prices that are particularly moderate. For instance, many pieces can be bought for as little as 50c or 75c each. (Prices slightly higher in the West.)

For further information about Glacier, write Fostoria Glass Company, Moundsville, W. Va.

THE GLASS OF FASHION

Fostoria **GLACIER**

May 1936 ad shows Fostoria Glacier, the Sun-Ray pattern with bands of acid etched or satinized decoration. Note that Fenton and others were making clear, acid decorated wares at this same time

Line 5082, Fostoria Glass Co. Six sided green stem water goblet, clear spiral optic bowl, 7 ³⁄₄ inches, $18-20; liquor cocktail panel optic with unknown gray hand cutting, 4 ¹⁄₂ inches, $12-16. Produced 1924-1943.

55

Fairfax pattern #2375, Fostoria Glass Co. After dinner cup, 2 ¾ inches and saucer 4 ¾ inches diameter, green, $20-24. Compote, green, 6 ½ inches, $25-30. 1927-1941.

Fostoria entered into the Glass Menagerie business along with almost every other American glass house circa 1940. This ad from *Crockery and Glass Journal* dates from May 1940.

Fern pattern, Fostoria Glass Co. Lemon Plate with plate etching #501, black/"ebony" with gold edge decoration, 1929-1932, 8 ½ inches diameter at handles, $36-42.

June 1941 ad shows Fostoria's Orchid sand etched pattern. This was a popular decorating theme on crystal and china of the time by numerous manufacturers.

Hazel Atlas

In its time, Hazel Atlas Glass was one of "The Giants." I write above of Monongah glass as a major concern. Fenton and Fostoria Glass certainly made major contribution to the glass industry between the wars. Yet, it is Hazel Atlas that by any measures dwarfs all other West Virginia glass concerns.

So why is little, almost nothing, written about Hazel Atlas? There are several reasons. It was purchased by a larger concern and the archives have not survived, thus there is no working paper history. It made truly everyday objects. Glass for homes, canning, items given away with cereal or flour, and objects of glass we used, threw away, and paid little mind to. Hazel Atlas made them by the tens of thousands, literally by the millions. And it made them in factories all over America. The story of Hazel Atlas is one of a giant national corporation, a company so large its story is difficult to grasp.

Hazel Atlas is of extreme importance to West Virginia because the corporate headquarters were always in Wheeling, West Virginia. From West Virginia the orders were placed, directives given, and decisions made. Hazel Atlas, at its peak, operated twelve plants at once, although fourteen different plants were utilized over the course of time.

In 1928, shortly before the eve of the depression, Hazel Atlas had annual sales of $25,466,000. In 1928 one million dollars was an immense amount. This twenty-five million dollars was created by eleven thousand railroad box cars of glassware being shipped all over the world. In 1927 and 1930 Hazel Atlas claimed *Over One Billion Pieces* of glass sold annually. That is IMMENSE.

The 1930s Hazel Atlas tableware and kitchenware color spectrum included colorless crystal, amber, milk glass or opal, green, pink, black, and blue (collectors call it Cobalt). Dating color production periods is difficult at best. Some hints include a trade journal quote from *China, Glass and Lamps* noted in May of 1929 that "as their first major incursion into the field of transparent colored glass, the Hazel Atlas Co., of Wheeling, announces a line of mixing bowls in green glass." These were initially made at the Washington, Pennsylvania, factory, but catalogs note shortly thereafter they were shipped from Clarksburg. The shipping point for glass, a heavy product, can safely be understood as its point of manufacture in this context. In 1935 coverage stated "pink glassware is offered in the line of Hazel Atlas . . . this, the maker claims, is the first time they have done pink glassware." (*Crockery and Glass Journal* September 1935)

In West Virginia, Wheeling served as the corporate office and as home to their metal cap and closure factory. No Hazel Atlas glass was made in Wheeling. From the company's inception in 1902, the Clarksburg, West Virginia, plant produced tumblers. It had been organized as The Republic Glass Co. to make tumblers, a daily living staple in a pre-plastic or pre-Styrofoam cup world. The Clarksburg plant was developed to adapt machines to make tumblers, a very specialized use, which had until then been made by time consuming hand blown glass methods. The Clarksburg plant was to remain predominately a tumbler and tableware factory as long as it operated as Hazel Atlas. In 1912 it already had grown to 400 employees. A company catalog dated 1929 states that the "tumbler plant (at Clarksburg) occupies 15 acres of floor space and employs 1200 people." *China, Glass and Lamps* states the Clarksburg site was being expanded to accommodate increased demand for "table glassware and tumblers which are made exclusively at this factory." (June 1929)

Earlier, in 1916, Hazel Atlas opened a factory in Grafton, West Virginia. This factory operated until "H-A" was purchased by Continental Can in 1960. Predominately jars (glass containers with wide mouths) were manufactured in Grafton. In a similar fashion, the large Hazel Atlas plants at Washington, Pennsylvania, were largely dedicated to opal (milk glass) bottles and to other clear and colored jars and containers. In the Hazel Atlas corporate structure, each factory specialized in various types of production. Today one way to discern what was made at different H-A factories is by the notes indicating where products were shipped from in the original catalogs.

When looking at Hazel Atlas tableware, the names for Hazel Atlas patterns are often collector/author generated and not factory names. A short checklist of some popular Hazel Atlas tableware patterns from between the world wars would include:

Aurora
Cloverleaf
Colonial Block
Florentine No. 1 (or Poppy No. 1)
Florentine No. 2 (or Poppy No. 2)
Fruits
Little Hostess Party Dishes (children's dishes)
Moderntone
New Century
Newport (or Hairpin)
Ovide
Ribbon
Roxana
Royal Lace
Starlight

Few specific mentions to Hazel Atlas lines are found in trade journals. In 1934, an exhibit of "a beautiful new line of Platonite Dinnerware" was included in an exhibit in Chicago (*China, Glass and Lamps* July 1934). In 1936, Platonite was defined for us "Platonite, the new milky white dinnerware by Hazel Atlas Glass Co." and noted it "features the Newport design which is most pleasant." (*China, Glass and Lamps* July 1936)

Other very popular lines produced by Hazel Atlas were not offered in the necessary shapes to complete table settings. An example is Criss Cross, a kitchen pattern in mixing bowls, butter dishes, covered refrigerator dishes, etc. but not plates or serving pieces. While several authors have used dates for these and other Hazel Atlas patterns, I have been unable to find the source for such dates and believe some to be incorrect. Until further information is available, it would only be wise to say most of the above patterns were introduced from the early 1930s or later and that few colored, other than milk glass, lines remained in production after the early 1940s. Several authors questioned reported they had relied on the dates used by earlier authors. One author has said the dates from an earlier book were used but a year added or subtracted here and there to avoid the appearance of copying another's work. This calls into question most reported Hazel Atlas tableware data without specific proofs. Further intriguing is the attribution by glass authors of some patterns to both Hazel Atlas factories in Clarksburg, West Virginia, and to the company factory in Zanesville, Ohio. Hazel Atlas had acquired an old glass factory in Zanesville in 1920.

Over fourteen different Hazel Atlas glass catalogs from the between the wars period have been surveyed, several having over 200 illustrated pages. Two things from the catalogs seem most interesting: no extensive listing of the tableware patterns are shown in any of the catalogs and none of the listed "tableware" or tumbler products were being shipped (F.O.B.) from any point other than Clarksburg. This is not to say that the popular patterns were all made in Clarksburg but to note that little information is available and what does exist points to Clarksburg. In describing the Clarksburg plant in 1933, *China, Glass and Lamps* said "being the world's largest tumbler factory, this plant also produces varied lines of table glassware." (November 1933) No trade journal mentions of tableware production from Zanesville were found. Five catalogs, all dating to the 1920s, say explicitly "tumbler and glassware factory located in Clarksburg, W.Va." What was happening in the 1930s, when the Hazel Atlas story is most complex and intriguing, remains unanswered.

Hazel Atlas Glass Co. Original factory morgue pieces from Clarksburg, West Virginia, factory, labels intact, Ritz blue open lace edge # 9644 plate, 8 ¼ inches, $35-45 without label; Aurora pattern #9642 bowl, 2 ¼ inches, $12-16 without label.

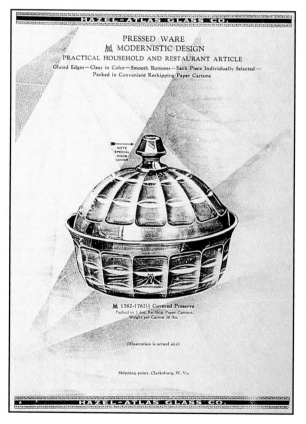

Hazel Atlas catalog illustration, circa late 1920s. Note shipping point, "Clarksburg, W.Va." and the "H-A" trademark is visible in the drawing to appear on the object's bottom. The caption names this piece a "covered preserve" and in a design or pattern then called "Modernistic." It was available then in clear only but was later produced in depression era green, milk or opal glass, and possibly other colors. *Catalog image from Corning Museum of Glass, Rakow Library.*

HAZEL-ATLAS GLASS CO.

PRESSED WARE
⒣ MODERNISTIC DESIGN
HALL BOY JUG

Glazed Edges—Clear in Color—Smooth Bottoms—Each Individually Selected
Packed in Convenient Reshipping Paper Cartons

NOTE
SMOOTH
FINISHED
HANDLE

(Illustration is actual size)

⒣ 13025 HALL BOY JUG
Capacity 3 pints
Packed in 1 doz. Re-Ship. Paper Cartons
Weight per Carton 36 lbs.

Shipping point, Clarksburg, W. Va.

PRESSED WARE
⒣ MODERNISTIC DESIGN

⒣ 13001 Spooner
Packed in 3 doz.
Re-Ship. Paper Cartons
Weight per Carton 39 lbs.

⒣ 1738-1738½ Covered Butter
Packed in 3 doz. Re-Ship. Paper Cartons
Weight per Carton, 62 lbs.

PRACTICAL
HOUSEHOLD
AND RESTAURANT
ARTICLES

Glazed Edges—Clear in Color—
Smooth Bottoms—Each Piece
Individually Selected—Packed
in Convenient Reshipping
Paper Cartons.

(Illustrations are actual size)

NOTE
SPECIAL
KNOB
COVER

Shipping point, Clarksburg, W. Va.

WHEELING, WEST VIRGINIA

Left: Hazel Atlas catalog illustration circa late 1920s. Note shipping point, "Clarksburg, W.Va." Caption calls this object a "Hall Boy Jug" HA # 13025 and notes capacity as 3 pints. *Catalog image from Corning Museum of Glass, Rakow library.*

Right: Hazel Atlas catalog illustration circa late 1920s. Note shipping point, "Clarksburg, W.Va." Caption names objects as Modernistic Spooner HA #13001 and Covered butter HA #1738. *Catalog image from Corning Museum of Glass, Rakow library.*

Chevron pattern Hazel Atlas cream, 3 ¼ inches and sugar 3 inches. Perhaps the most produced and recognized of all H-A Clarksburg products. $26-38 pair.

Over One Billion Pieces
of these Articles Sold
Annually by

Hazel-Atlas Glass Co.

Ash Trays	Medicine Glasses
Battery Jars	Mixing Bowls
Berry Sets	Mustard Jars
Bird Baths	Nappies
Butter Dishes	Narrow-Neck Bottles
Candy Jars	Ointment and Salve Jars
Caster Cups	Olive Bottles
Cherry Bottles	Packers Tumblers
Coasters	Paste Jars
Cold Cream Jars	Panels
Creamers	Percolater Tops
Cruets	Pickle Bottles
Crushed Fruit Jars	Pomade Bottles
Egg Cups	Quinine Bottles
Eye Cups	Radio Battery Jars
Fountain Tumblers	Refrigerator Sets
Fruit Jars	Salt Dips
Glue Bottles	Shakers
Hotel Tumblers	Sherbets
Ice Tea Tumblers	Shoe Polish Bottles
Ink Bottles	Soap Slabs
Jam Jars	Sugar Bowls
Jars	Sundry Glassware
Jelly Glasses	Syrups
Jugs	Table Tumblers
Malted Milk Bottles	Tail Light Cups
Massage Cream Jars	Talcum Jars
Measuring Cups	

Flint, Amber, Opal and Blue Glass

Look for the ⒣ Mark of Quality

HAZEL-ATLAS GLASS COMPANY
WHEELING, W. VA.

Sales Offices in all Principal Cities
Ten Factories

1929

Hazel Atlas One Billion piece ad from *China and Glass Directory* of 1929 for Hazel Atlas includes the objects then made at their "ten factories."

Hazel Atlas Glass. Furniture coaster with HA logo mark, label says "Hazel-Atlas Glass Co. Wheeling, W.Va. item G-2546 Shop #8 35 per minute 11-10-32," green, 3 inches. With label $18-20; without label $2-3. *Dane Moore collection.*

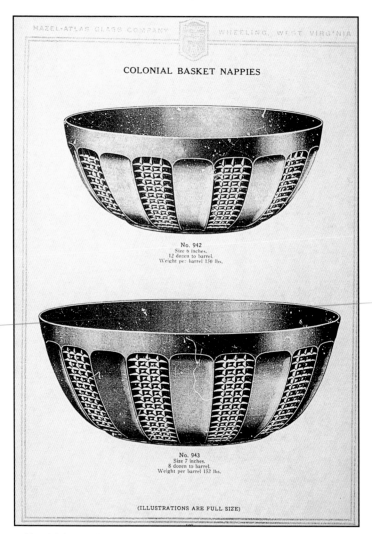

Hazel Atlas catalog illustration circa late 1920s, but not the same catalog as used above. Caption calls these nappies, the old English word for round bowls. The pattern is clearly announced to be "Colonial Basket." *Catalog image from Corning Museum of Glass, Rakow library.*

Shirley Temple Hazel Atlas handled mug. Cobalt blue, 3 ½ inches. Part of the breakfast premium set of bowl, mug, and small milk pitcher. $25-35. Heavily reproduced in an array of unflattering bad copies.

Clover Pattern, Hazel Atlas Glass Co. Cups in green, $10-12; black, $18-24; and clear, $6-8.

This is the cover to a dated 1939 Hazel Atlas *Book of Recipes*. While the booklet is heavy on canning jar illustrations and recipes, it includes kitchen and tableware glass illustrations. The cover features a berry set about to be employed. The crystal pattern has been named "Starlight" by collectors.

Ribbed tumbler, Hazel Atlas Glass Co. Carried from factory by author's great aunt, HA employee in Clarksburg, to his grandmother. Cobalt blue, 3 ¼ inches, $16-22.

This jug and tumbler set is from the 1939 Hazel Atlas *Book of Recipes*. Shown is the ribbed tumbler and ball jug in what appears to be a variety of color decorations.

Hazel Atlas catalog illustration circa late 1920s. Note shipping point, "Clarksburg, W.Va." This is the Colonial Design candy jar H-A # 3055 (item 3055 ½ would be the lid). *Catalog image from Corning Museum of Glass, Rakow library.*

Hazel Atlas Glass Co. Amethyst individual crimped berry bowl, 4 ¾ inches, $12-16; cobalt blue master berry bowl, 9 inches, $20-24; clear individual beaded rim and stippled berry bowl, 4 ½ inches, $4-8; green master crimped berry bowl, 9 inches, $14-20. The last only has the H over A company mark in the bottom center.

Hazel Atlas clear commemoratives. Simpson Creek Baptist Church sauce or jelly bowl, 1 ½ inches tall x 4 inches diameter, $25-35; coaster "Visit Clarksburg, HA (logo) W.VA.," ¾ inches tall x 3 ¼ inches diameter, $16-20; sauce or jelly bowl "compliments of Hazel-Atlas Glass Co. John W. Davis Day Aug 11-24 Clarksburg, W.Va.," 1 ½ inches tall x 4 inches diameter. Latter given at parade in Davis's honor after unsuccessful run for Vice President of the United States. Scarce, $80-100.

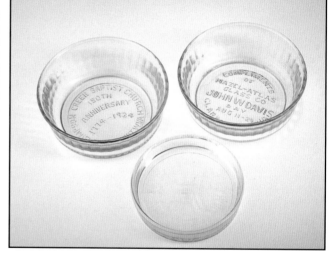

Hazel Atlas Glass Co. Royal Lace pattern green open sugar bowl, 4 inches, $18-22; Ritz blue sherbet, 2 ¾ inches, $35-45.

Ritz blue, Hazel Atlas Glass Co. Criss Cross pattern, ¼ lb. Butter with lid, 6 ½ inches length, $150-160; beater jar manufactured for sales with metal lid and egg beater label says item #9659 original factory sample with label, 4 ¼ inches, $60-80 without label or beater; salt shaker with "HA" on base, black bakelite cap, 3 inches, $12-16; heavy tumbler #553 marked "HA" on base, original Clarksburg factory sample with labels, 4 inches, $15-20 without labels.

Huntington Tumbler

Huntington Tumbler Company was organized in 1900 by Anthony Zihlman and others in Huntington, West Virginia. Production began mid-year 1901. Mr. Zilhman was a practical glass man, having been a native of Switzerland where he entered the glass industry. He came to the U.S. in 1866 and began working glass in Bellaire, Ohio. In 1881 he and his brother Joseph were the organizers of the Cumberland Glass Works in Cumberland, Maryland. After relocating to Huntington, Zihlamn served as President of Huntington Tumbler until his death in 1912. The sons of Edward Zilhman's ran the factory after this death: Edward L. Zilhamn was President, Charles Zilhman was Vice President, and William Zihlman ran the decorating department.

In 1900 the West Virginia Bureau of Labor inspected Huntington Tumbler and reported a monthly payroll of $5,600 with 90 male and 30 female employees, for a total employment of 120. This is a slightly larger than average size tableware plant for this time period. In 1923 the factory products were described as "tumblers, goblets, bar glassware, tankards, nappies, and a general line of lead-blown tableware." The National Glass Budget reported in 1927 (15 January) that Huntington Tumbler's exhibit at the Pittsburgh show included "high grade crystal and colored glassware, two-toned stemware and tumblers."

In 1928 advertisements list the line as noted above for the year before but have added beverage sets, console sets, candy jars, and the ever ambiguous "specialties." Decorations available in 1928 included light cutting, needle etching, gold, iridescent, lusters, color treatments, crackled ware, and two-tone stems. That same year Huntington introduced a line with octagonal bowls, responding to the European influence calling for "straight and angular lines in keeping with the mode in modern art and design and architecture." This was from the rural hills of West Virginia! Note also that 1928 ads list only crystal, green, amber, and rose. In 1931 Huntington Tumbler ads mention a "complete line of lead crystal, or two-tone combinations of green, rose, amber, amethyst, Ritz blue, or Topaz with crystal. That embraces just about the entire glass color pallet of the 1920-1930s!

Huntington Tumbler closed in 1932.

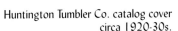

Huntington Tumbler Co. catalog cover circa 1920-30s.

Huntington Tumbler Co. catalog cover circa 1910-20s.

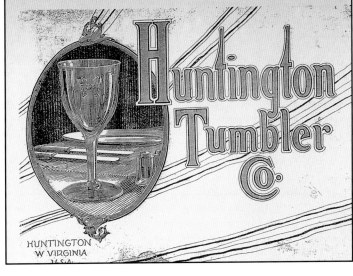

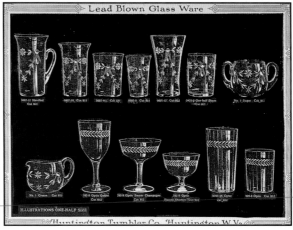

Hand cut Huntington Tumbler from the circa 1910-20s catalog. Note the form of the handled ice tea, which appears as a photo below.

Hand cut Huntington Tumbler from the circa 1910-20s catalog. Sugar and creamer forms appear in this and the illustration above.

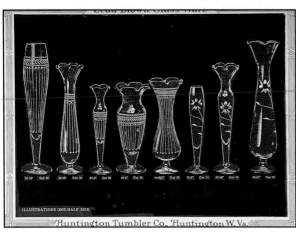

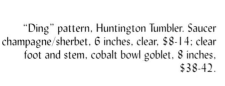

Hand cut Huntington Tumbler from the circa 1910-20s catalog. Familiar shaped vases, made by perhaps every handmade glass plant, here include hand cuttings that appear to be distinctive to Huntington Tumbler.

"Ding" pattern, Huntington Tumbler. Saucer champagne/sherbet, 6 inches, clear, $8-14; clear foot and stem, cobalt bowl goblet, 8 inches, $38-42.

Huntington Tumbler. All clear foot and stem with green bowl. Iced tea, 6 ¼ inches, $14-20; cordial, 4 inches, $28-34; optic bowl saucer champagne/sherbet, 6 inches, $12-18.

Huntington Tumbler ad from *Pottery, Glass & Brass Salesman* 1925 showing #772 covered bulbous jug and a tumbler in crackle glass and an hour glass form covered jug #771 with a diamond optic. Both are noted as available in optic or crackle treatments and in crystal, amber, or iridescent.

Vases, Huntington Tumbler. Fan vase, optic, green, 9 inches, $38-48; three lobed "Clover vase" #23, green, 9 inches, $40-50. *West Virginia Museum of American Glass collection.*

Hand tinted Huntington Tumbler catalog page circa 1920s shows amber, green, and pink fan vases with varying hand cut decorations. The #20 console set is shown here undecorated.

Huntington Tumbler hand tinted catalog page circa 1920s includes the #23 Clover Vase illustrated above, a third form for sugar and creamers, and a ringed stemware line designated #225.

Handled ice teas, Huntington Tumbler. Optic bowl handled ice tea, all green, $12-18; and pink optic bowl with crystal handle, $16-20; both 5 ½ inches.

Huntington Tumbler forms. Stem shapes all shown elsewhere herein, are here in clear and with cuttings that may or may not be Huntington Tumbler work. Molds and thus shapes were continued in production by Dunbar Glass in clear after Huntginton Tumbler closed. Footed tumbler, 6 ¾ inches, $14-18; Ding cordial, 5 inches, $22-28; parfait, 7 ¼ inches, $12-16.

Huntington Tumbler saucer champagne/sherbet, clear foot and stem, ruby bowl, 6 ¼ inches, $24-28.

Huntington Tumbler. Iced tea, clear foot, optic, amber bowl, 6 ¼ inches, $14-18; goblet, clear foot and bowl, optic, pink bowl, 7 ¾ inches, $24-28; parfait, clear foot and stem, cobalt blue bowl, 7 ½ inches, $26-32.

Huntington Tumbler optic bowl and pressed stem in sherbet, goblet, tall sherbet, or saucer champagne, wine, iced tea, and cocktail forms. Photo source unknown.

Huntington Tumbler clear square foot with green bowl low goblet, $12-18; clear stepped square foot low goblet with unknown etching (etch may not be Huntington Tumbler), $12-18.

A 1928 Huntington Tumbler ad was a full page in *China, Glass & Lamps* as they prepared for the Pittsburgh 1929 trade show. Shown is an elaborate cut #975 but it is the exhaustive listing of treatments, colors, and decorations that is unexpected.

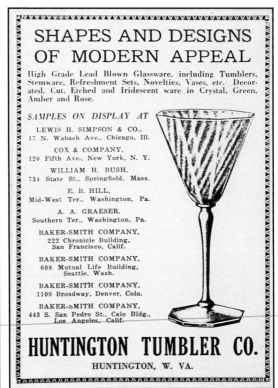

China, Glass & Lamps ad from November 1928 illustrates and allows us to document the octagonal stemware shown above.

Huntington Tumbler. Goblet, green stem and foot, clear octagonal bowl, 8 inches, $30-38.

Huntington Tumbler compote, green with optic, 10 inch diameter, 4 ¾ inches tall, $38-46.

Huntington Tumbler ad from The Pottery, Glass & Brass Salesman December 1925. The extensive treatments offered shown challenge any collector today.

Louie Glass Co.

Few companies, in the glass industry or elsewhere, are largely the story of one person. But it appears the early history of Louie Glass is best told as the story of Louie, the man.

Louie Wohinc died in Weston, West Virginia, in 1950 at age sixty-two. He was born in Austria and at the age of nine entered a glass factory to learn the trade. He worked sixteen hours a day. An uncle persuaded him to come to America at age fifteen. Upon his arrival, he worked in Rochester, Pennsylvania, before moving to Tiffin, Ohio. He next went to Huntington, West Virginia, to work glass and then on to Weston, West Virginia. He left Weston, where he worked in a milk bottle factory, moving then to Buckhannon, West Virginia. In 1919, he returned to Weston and, with associates, organized the first Weston Glass Co. Louie's story of travel and working in a multitude of factories remained typical of glass workers as late as the 1950s.

In 1926, he started Louie Glass, which operated until 1996 as Louie Glass, then continued as Louie Glass, a subsidiary of Princess House Glass, and since 2000 has operated as Glass Works WV. Louie was a major character in American hand made glass. He started the West Virginia Glass Specialty Company in 1929. In 1940 he opened the Ludwick Glass Company of Glenville, West Virginia, and in 1944 he opened a new Weston Glass Co. (the original having burned years before). In 1945 he opened The Huntington Glass Company at Kenova, West Virginia.

In the period following the First World War, he established a reputation for being the champion glass blower in America. In 1932 he was credited with "being able to blow more stemware in a single shift than any other man has ever blown." It was told that his operations of a factory from the beginning was unorthodox but that his enthusiasm for salesmanship sold glassware and brought a big demand for it. His early efforts were with worker owned cooperative glasshouses. Later his companies were operated as traditional corporations.

Besides creating a major empire of glass factories, Louie's factories were, again like Hobbs Glass over a century before, spawning grounds for others who acquired a skill and were motivated to move on. Lewis County Glass Co, Pennsboro Glass, Mid-Atlantic Glass, and others were formed by ex-Louie employees.

About the products of Louie Glass we know a considerable amount. The company's early glass included color: Cobalt blue, black amethyst, rose (pink), green, and crystal. A 1932 *China, Glass and Lamps* advertisement shows stemmed goblets, a 7 ½ inch octagonal plate, and 6 and 8 inch round plates. The text states "All shapes are made in rose, green, and our new crystal glass, a metal of exceptional excellence." An undated advertisement shows Louie Glass company "stemless stemware" and pictures lily pad feet of black amethyst on colorless bowls. Further the items are offered in plain, cut, etched, and rock crystal effects! Rock crystal effects are generally deep cut and polished designs. This same shape, the lily pad foot, is known to have also been made by Seneca, McBride, and Fry Glass companies. However, all but McBride and Louie used lead crystal. Louie and McBride glass was a soda lime formula. I believe Louie lily pads exist with depression green, ruby, or black feet.

An existing Louie catalogue shows an amazing variety, including one page of elegant black amethyst in twenty-four shapes! Pages of pitchers (jugs to the trade) with hand applied handles can be found in colorless, black amethyst, Cobalt blue, rose pink, and "depression" green. Some of those same shapes can be found in ruby. It is the current belief that Louis Glass did not make ruby. However, Louie, the man, did! Commonly told stories in Weston are of an order placed with the interconnected Louie companies being made at one factory one time and at another when next ordered. The moulds were transferred by truck from factory to factory to best accommodate production schedules. Thus, many shapes cannot be attributed to any specific Weston company if it was one of the factories originally associated with Louie Wohinc. They may in deed be Weston Glass Co., or Louie Glass, or West Virginia Glass Specialty Co. . . . or all three depending on the orders needed at the time and the availability of production facilities at one of the three factories.

Some elegant stem lines should be attributed to Louie Glass as the catalogue pages show. These are found in colorless, in Cobalt, and ruby with colorless stem and foot, and with depression green stems and feet. The same shapes were produced in Weston later with Cobalt blue and black feet on colorless stems and bowls. Pink is likely as well, but I have yet to hold any in my hand. Recalling the advertisement above for lily pad feet, it is probable that these were also available with cuttings, etching, etc. from the factory.

The repeal of prohibition had a significant impact on Louie, both as a single factory and as the man's empire. Bar ware, the type of production best suited for mouth blown and hand formed glassware, the type all of Louie's factories made, was in need again! It seems probable that all color production ceased in the summer of 1940. The factory went out on strike and when the strike was settled, due to war restrictions on materials or changes in consumer taste, color was never again a major element of

Louie Glass production. It is possible some handles or feet were made in color after this date, but no large or solid colored objects.

It should also be noted that glass that sells well quickly has imitators. It is difficult to ascertain when Louie led the trends and when they followed. It is likely some of both. It is noteworthy that some pitcher shapes in Cobalt made by Cambridge Glass are very similar to Louie products, as are certain tall flared vases in color and colorless. Ringed tumblers from the Weston factories look very much like those produced by Imperial, Morgantown, and others. While many Louie and Weston shapes are distinctive, be alert to possible look-alike shapes produced by other glass houses.

When Louie died in 1950, the management of Louie Glass passed to his unmarried daughter, Margaret Wohinc. She served as company president and directed the affairs of the company until her retirement and the sale of the company in 1972. Women in the glass industry were uncommon in any capacity then and her ability to maintain the company for such a long period is a major testimony to a capable person working under what must have been often trying circumstances. The Wohinc influence was, for two generations, a significant and major force in American handmade glass.

Vase, Louie Glass Co. and possibly West Virginia Glass Specialty Co. "Iron mold" shapes, mouth blown into rigid iron mold for shape, 9 inches, $28-34; 6 inches, $16-22.

Jug with cover, Louie Glass and possibly Weston Glass. Green jug with black applied handle and pressed lid, 10 ¼ inches to top of jug, $80-95.

Variations from one mold/shape, Louie Glass Co. Two ring base shape, cobalt blue with crimped top, two reeded handles as urn, etched "Atlantic City," $85-100; same mold in clear with crimped top and two plain applied handles (uncommon in clear), $40-60; black amethyst vase, $45-65. All 9 ½ inches. Note this is the same mold/shape as the covered jug in the opposite image.

Louie Glass and Weston Glass Co. Forms shown in 1920-30s catalogs where the catalog page tops cites both companies. Green foot, pink pulled stem and bowl. Sherbet, panel optic with hand gray cut, 5 ½ inches; water goblet, diamond optic bowl, 7 inches; liquor cocktail, 4 ¾ inches; sherbet or saucer champagne, gray cut band and diamond optic, 5 ¼ inches; iced tea with gray hand cutting, 5 inches. All $12-20 each.

Louie Glass Co. Vase #56 with crimped top, black amethyst, $12-14; orchid (made briefly in mid-1930s), $12-16; and cobalt blue, $10-14. All 5 inches

Louie Glass and West Virginia Glass Specialty. Stems, clear foot and "hokey pokey" six sided stem with ruby bowl, water goblet, 8 ¼ inches, $28-36; sherbet or saucer champagne, 6 ½ inches, $16-24; liquor cocktail, 5 ¼ inches, $16-24; iced tea, clear foot and stem with cobalt blue bowl and platinum banding, 6 ¼ inches, $18-26.

Louie Glass Co. ad October 1932 includes tableware and the notice of "new crystal glass." Only colored wares were made in the early years.

Green stemware, Louie Glass Co. Green foot and "hokey pokey" stem with colorless optic bowl, tall sherbet or saucer champagne, 6 ¾ inches, $12-16; green foot and stem with green "hokey pokey" stem, colorless optic bowl, and hand cut gray decoration, 4 ½ inches, $12-16.

"Hokey Pokey" stemware, Louie Glass Co. Clear optic bowl with green feet and "hokey pokey" stem, goblet with unidentified gray hand cutting, 8 ¼ inches, $18-22; liquor cocktail with unidentified gray hand cutting, 5 inches, $12-14.

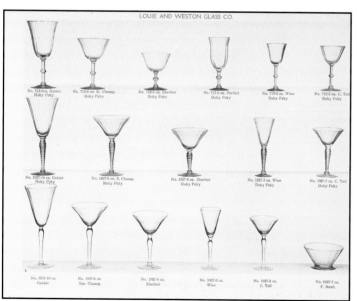

Louie and Weston Glass catalog page Stemware lines #712 with a single knop, line 1927 (probably also the year of introduction for this stem) and a crystal hand pulled ladies leg stem. The appearance of crystal may date this catalog to circa 1932 or shortly thereafter.

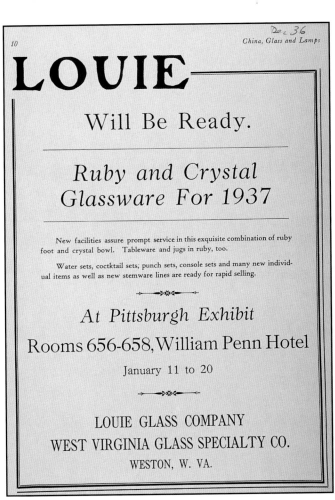
Louie Glass ad from December 1936 promoting Ruby and Crystal for 1937. Note the bottom of the page mentions both Louie and West Virginia Glass Specialty Co.

Vases, Louie Glass Co. cobalt vase sold by another company that added a white metal stand, $26-32; same form in black amethyst, glass only 8 inches, $22-28.

Louie Glass Co. Six sided "hokey pokey" stems. Green foot and stem with clear diamond optic bowl, 6 ¼ inches, $12-18; clear foot and stem with cobalt bowl, 5 ¾ inches, $14-22; pink foot and stem with diamond optic bowl, 5 ½ inches, $12-18.

Louie and/or Weston Glass syrup pitcher, pink body with green applied handle and green lid, 4 ¼ inches to top of pitcher, $32-40.

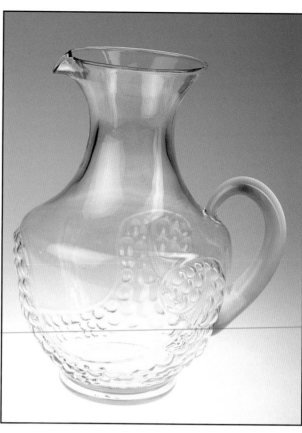

Ivy Balls, Louie Glass and/or West Virginia Glass Specialty. Clear foot and stem, ruby bowl and gold bands, crimped top, 6 ½ inches, $40-48; cobalt blue crimped top ivy ball, 5 inches, $25-30; clear foot and stem cobalt bowl crimped top, 6 ½ inches, $35-45.

Louis Glass Co. iron mold clear pitcher with applied handle. Made in cobalt in the 1930s in this and a smaller size and as late as the 1960s in clear. 9 inches, $25-35.

Louie Glass clear jug with applied reeded handle, $20-30; and cobalt body with clear applied reeded handle, $65-85; both 7 ¼ inches. Cobalt blue tumbler, 3 ¾ inches, $12-14. Note: this flat form was also made by Cambridge Glass. The author has yet to learn how to distinguish the cobalt versions. The form appears in Weston area catalogs through the 1960s in clear/crystal.

Black Amethyst vases, Louie Glass Co. An example of the amazing variety of forms made in small bud styled vases in Weston. Footed vase, 9 ¾ inches; bulbous ringed, 8 ¾ inches; bud vase, 7 inches; vase, 7 ¾ inches; vase, 8 inches; vase, 7 ¾ inches; vase, 7 inches. All $12-22 each.

Jug #455, Louie Glass Co. Ruby jug, 10 oz., rings at neck with clear applied reeded handle, illustrated in 1937 trade journal ads and noted it as a shape "we have offered for some time," 6 ¾ inches, $80-95.

Louie Glass and/ or Weston Glass Co. Pinch decanter, ruby with clear stopper shown in 1920-30s catalogs, 7 ¾ inches to top of decanter, $80-95.

Louie Glass Co. Ruby with clear foot bud vase, 9 ¾ inches, $28-36; vase, 11 inches, $48-60; shallow compote, 4 inches x 6 ¾ inches diameter, $38-50.

Vases, Louie Glass Co. cobalt iron mold patterned vase, 9 ½ inches, $48-65; jug from vase mold adapted with one clear reeded handle and ice lip to become cobalt jug, 9 inches, $75-85; vase mold with two reeded handles and top left smooth to become urn, black amethyst, 9 ¼ inches, $100-120. Last form not verified as Weston area but attributed to. Note: any mold used for body of vase could be a vase, jug, or urn. All made prior to June 1940.

Queen Alfreda I . . . Miss Alfreda Dutton

Program cover from a Weston area glass festival held in 1938. The images in the program are sources for attribution and are supported by ads and catalog illustrations. The cover image is a color footed stem line with hand cutting, very typical of the Weston area production.

Page from inside the Glass Exposition program showing Queen Alfreda sitting on her throne of crystal. All local and largely colored ware. Note the abundance of cocktail shaker forms.

Louie and/or Weston Glass. #2 Decanter, ruby with clear stopper, 12 inches, $55-65; cocktail shaker, ruby with chrome lid, 9 inches to top of glass (chrome lids varied with time of production), $60-75.

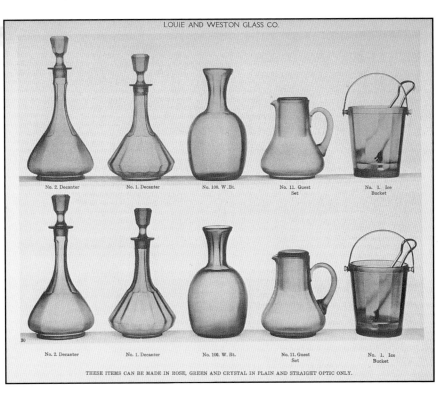

No. 2. Decanter   No. 1. Decanter   No. 100. W.Bt.   No. 11. Guest Set   No. 1. Ice Bucket

No. 2. Decanter   No. 1. Decanter   No. 100. W. Bt.   No. 11. Guest Set   No. 1. Ice Bucket

THESE ITEMS CAN BE MADE IN ROSE, GREEN AND CRYSTAL IN PLAIN AND STRAIGHT OPTIC ONLY.

Louie and Weston catalog page from circa early 1930s showing #2 decanter illustrated above and one form for a locally made pressed ice buckets.

Ice bucket, Weston Glass. Clear with pressed panel optic and hand cutting. Attributed to Cataract Sharpe cutting firm of Weston circa 1930s. 7 inches, $75-95.

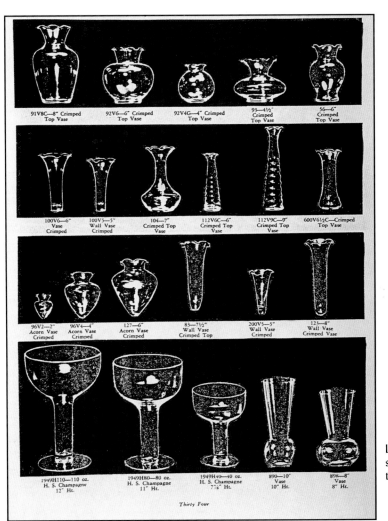

91V8C—8" Crimped Top Vase   92V6—6" Crimped Top Vase   92V4G—4" Crimped Top Vase   93—4½" Crimped Top Vase   56—6" Crimped Top Vase

100V6—6" Vase Crimped   100V5—5" Wall Vase Crimped   104—7" Crimped Top Vase   112V6C—6" Crimped Top Vase   112V9C—9" Crimped Top Vase   600V6½C—Crimped Top Vase

96V2—2" Acorn Vase Crimped   96V4—4" Acorn Vase Crimped   127—6" Acorn Vase Crimped   83—7½" Wall Vase Crimped Top   200V5—5" Wall Vase Crimped   123—8" Wall Vase Crimped Vase

1949H110—110 oz. H. S. Champagne 12" Ht.   1949H80—80 oz. H. S. Champagne 11" Ht.   1949H40—40 oz. H. S. Champagne 7½" Ht.   890—10" Vase 10" Ht.   898—8" Vase 8" Ht.

Thirty Four

Louie catalog page from circa 1960s shows that forms and shapes used in the 1920s-40s remained active for a very long time. Note: acorns and vase #56 shown above.

Mid-Atlantic

In 1937, during a labor strike at Louie Glass Co. in Weston, Loy Casto, a Louie Company glassworker, was traveling along US Route 50 and saw an abandoned, concrete building. It looked capable of supporting the intense heat and needs of a small glass plant. And that was the mission he was on: looking for a place to commence independent operations of a glasshouse.

Shortly thereafter, eleven glass workers from Louie Glass opened as Mid-Atlantic Glass in Ellenboro, West Virginia, along the B&O Railroad and a few feet from US Route 50, a major east-west route. Each worker shared in the ownership. Products looked like what the men had been making previously, they used what skills they had and knew best. And it has worked for over fifty years.

Mouth blown and hand formed, colorless glass in the paste mould fashion represents the bulk of the millions of pieces produced by Mid-Atlantic. Paste Mold glass is mouth blown into a metal mold that imparts the object's shape. The name is derived from a paste spread inside the mold that allows the glassblower to turn the blowpipe and forming object, thus blurring and removing the unsightly mold seams. These creations are thin and seamless as final products. They are also labor intensive and require considerable skill. From 1937 until the early 1950s, Mid-Atlantic maintained, but perhaps not at all times, small tanks of colored glass for feet, handles, etc. to be applied to colorless bodies and vessels. In the late 1940s, Mid-Atlantic was shipping punch bowls, with depression or transparent green feet on the large colorless bowl and green handles on colorless punch cups, to Marshall Fields in Chicago . . . by the train car load! It was a great success there and as a product distributed elsewhere across America.

Mid-Atlantic is unknown to the world because its glass never bears its name. It is sold to distributors, decorating firms, and wholesalers who market it under their names. The company found it did not wish to compete with its own best customers. A recent company officer said "They do the selling and marketing and we concentrate on making it." Such has been the policy for decades.

However, with an average of 100 employees for six decades, the production has been immense. Colored feet and handles in green and ruby are the features that distinguish the more collectable products from the early decades. The same shapes and moulds are in many cases in use today. In 1987, the company transferred ownership from the original stockholders-founders (or their descendants) to new owners. Production continues at Mid-Atlantic Glass of West Virginia.

Mid-Atlantic Glass Co. Vase, clear crimp top with green foot, 6 ¼ inches, $12-16; green cordial, 2 ¾ inches, $14-18.

Monongah Glass Co.

One of my favorite factories is Monongah Glass Co. Early indications I found were that it had been a giant and had, simply with the selective telling of history, been neglected and forgotten. This is very much the truth. Monongah was, for three decades, a giant in the glass industry. I have in this book's opening essay told of the esteem in which Monongah glass and Northwood glass were held when both were new and competing in the market place. Please do not let these facts get away from you: around 1910 Monongah was an upper end, more expensive glass; it got top billing and name recognition in trade journals; and it was much larger than almost any of the factories we know by name and collect today.

So, let's try to capture a bit of the history, scale, and type of production of this alleged Giant.

Monongah Glass began operation in 1904 in an immense new factory in Fairmont, West Virginia. As Monongah grew it acquired two other glass factories in the city and operated all three of them. Production figures for 1908 cite 12,000 dozen glass articles every twenty-four hours, that's 144,000 items per day or roughly 4.5 million pieces of glass per month! By 1928 their success had made them vulnerable for takeover by the then huge Collins-Hocking glass empire and Monongha ceased to exist as a company. The Fairmont plant ceased operations circa 1933.

Monongah came into existence to utilize then new and emerging technology. The factory's organizers included H. L. Heintzelman, ex-superintendent at Rochester Glass Works in Pennsylvania, and William Moulds, with Rochester since 1872. A fire at the Rochester factory left the two temporarily unemployed and they saw opportunity in Fairmont, where several glass factories had already been operating for several years. Rochester had become a giant, employing 1,200 people, using great precision in crafting 75,000 dozen tumblers per week. But vacuum sealing was an emerging idea for food products (think of swanky swigs glasses filled with cheese or dried beef in jars like juice glasses). What happened at Monongah was seeing an opportunity and making connections. From the start Monongah had used continuous tank technology, not the then prevailing covered pots of small and limited capacity, to create its glass. In continuous tank production, the capacity was endless and many, many times greater than small single pots.

By 1910, Monongah joined with Beechnut Packing Company and an engineering firm in Hartford, Connecticut, to develop a mechanical feeder that pushed the glass into the moulds and an automatic press to form the objects. The speed with which objects were created soared. The new machines allowed the company to meet rigid standards for size, shape, and speed of production. A level of mechanical choreography never seen before in the glass industry was showcased, with great success, at Monongah.

If you are enchanted by the ideas and machinery behind glass production, two excellent sources that place the Monongah Glass advancements in their proper historical context are William A. Liddell's 1953 Dissertation at Yale entitled *The Development of Science in the American Glass Industry 1880-1904* (see especially pp. 153, 242-245). And "The New Factory of the Monongah Glass Company" by E. Ward Tillotson in the *American Ceramic Society Journal*, 4 (1921). The latter includes impressive photographs and drawings of the then newest factory. (I suspect it was this major new building campaign in 1921 that aided the Collins empire in gaining access to control of Monongah as Monongah struggled perhaps to pay for the new facility and its expensive machinery in the tighter money times of the late 1920s?)

In 1908 Monongah was shipping fifty-five boxcar loads of glass per month all over the US and to Canada, Mexico, Australia, South America, and beyond. At this time, on the eve of World War I, Monongah cataloged its wares as "pressed and blown tumblers and stem ware, needle etched, engraved, sand blasted, and decorated for family and bar trade." That list just about covers it all!

Two Monongah catalogues survive from circa 1910-early 1920s. These give some indication of the immensity of capacity. One illustrated and oversized catalogue has 326 pages, the other 300! Each page illustrates four to nine objects, mostly tumblers, in endless variety—plain, engraved, needle etched, and rich or brilliant cut. Included in these catalogues is an unexpected amount of pressed glass in imitation of cut glass.

To date, what little has been attributed to Monongah are those patterns show in *Weatherman's Colored Glassware of the Depression Era 2* (pages 275-279) where she shares original catalogue pages. Patterns that have become collectable resulting from her book include Bo Peep and Spring Time, and a distant third, called by Weatherman, "Roseland." The handmade Spring Time pattern time was adapted by Hocking Glass when it purchased Monongah Glass and became Hocking's very popular machine made "depression" Cameo pattern. Cameo is a pressed pattern with the molded in ballerina facing right and is often in colored glass. Spring Time, an acid etched decoration, is commonly found only in colorless glass and the ballerina faces left. One wonders why the change in direction?

Roseland, a plate etched decoration made by acid etching, is first shown in a 1915 trade journal advertisement. A 1916 dated Monongah catalogue supplement offers Roseland in thirty-six shapes. Roseland remains in the 1920s catalogue pages used in Weatherman. This suggests production spanning several years.

The company size and capacity were more than sufficient to produce a variety of patterns in large quantities. In 1917 the West Virginia Bureau of Labor inspected Monongah and reported 774 men and 29 women employees for a total employment of 803 people.

Color production entered Monongah's offering in the late 1920s: included were green, rose pink, amber, and crystal, often in combination. Several pressed stems appear applied to elegant hand blown thin bowls making the style of high end stemware then popular. One example of this combination of pressing and hand blowing might be called a Craig stem, named for the creator/patentee. Monongah in their literature called it only line #6102. This particular stem is of interest because it very closely resembles stems made in Morgantown, Weston, Tiffin, and perhaps others.

China, Glass and Lamps notes, January 22, 1923, that Monongah offered in their show room in Pittsburgh at the Fort Pitt "four new patterns of encrusted gold and flat gold decorated ware [which is] meeting with the approval of the buyers. Several new lines of ware, consisting of grape juice, lemonade, and a crackled glass water set are very popular."

The absorption of Monongah into the Hocking/Lancaster Glass conglomerate began in 1927. Heintzelman remained president of Monongah but I. T. Collins, Lancaster's president, was made Monongah's vice president. In April of 1927 a letter to the National Association of Manufacturers of Pressed and Blown Glassware, Monongah advised they were dismantling their tanks in Factory #1, "which were used in the production of hand ware." Further they stated that their tanks in Factory #6 were used "in making packers tumblers by machine," while the two tanks in Factory #3 were producing "bottles and opal ware on automatic machine." The end was near. During its almost three decades of active production Monongah seems to have included lines from hand made and elegant to machine mass produced and very utilitarian, all at the same time. What an immense undertaking.

A July 1927 notice in *Pottery, Glass and Brass Salesman* states: "As is generally known to the trade, the Lancaster Glass Company of Lancaster, Ohio, has taken over the handmade lines of Monongah Glass . . . and is offering complete lines of tableware, which includes Monongah stemware, etc., shown in the Lancaster colors." Bo-Peep is specifically noted as having been continued by Lancaster. Illustrated ads from the summer of 1927 show Monongah stems and etchings offered by The Hocking Glass Sales Corporation, representing Hocking-Lancaster and Standard Glass Companies. Worthy of note is that no ads showing Monongah stems and patterns under ANY name have been found after 1927.

By 1928 Monongah Glass appears in trade directories as a subsidiary of Turner Glass of Terre Haute, Indiana, a part of the Collins-Hocking empire. As late as 1933 Monongah appeared, for the very last time, as the Monongah Division of General Glass Corporation.

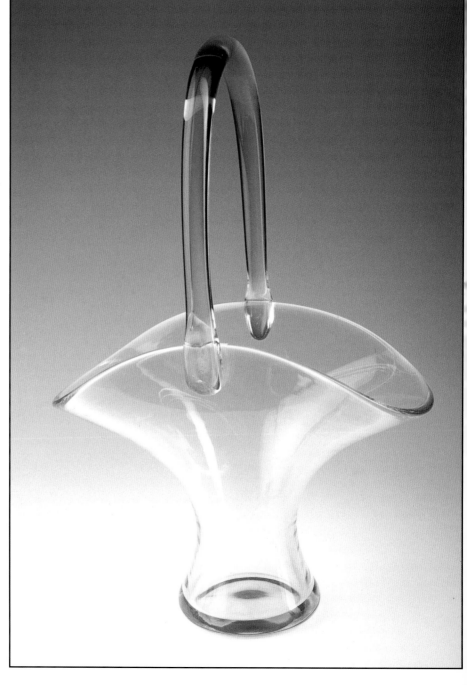

Basket, Monongah Glass Co. This example was carried home from the factory by a worker, 1924, and purchased from the family by the author in 1998. Pink, 14 ½ inches tall, $70-90.

No. 5—5, Cut 133, 42 oz.   No. 5—4, Cut 72, 31 oz.

Monongah Glass catalog page from the early 1900s shows lead glass, hand cut jugs. Monongah made high quality lead glass, cut in the Brilliant or Rich Cut style, and lighter styles as show here. This is page 303 from a massive oversized catalog of hundreds of shapes offered.

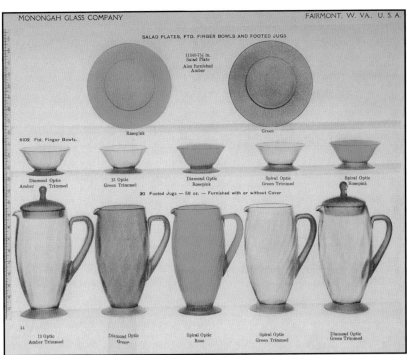

MONONGAH GLASS COMPANY   FAIRMONT, W. VA., U. S. A.

SALAD PLATES, FTD. FINGER BOWLS AND FOOTED JUGS

11340-7½ in.
Salad Plate
Also furnished
Amber

Rosepink   Green

6102 Ftd. Finger Bowls.

Diamond Optic   13 Optic   Diamond Optic   Spiral Optic   Spiral Optic
Amber Trimmed   Green Trimmed   Rosepink   Green Trimmed   Rosepink

20 Footed Jugs — 58 oz. — Furnished with or without Cover.

13 Optic   Diamond Optic   Spiral Optic   Spiral Optic   Diamond Optic
Amber Trimmed   Green   Rose   Green Trimmed   Green Trimmed

Monongah Glass colored catalog page circa 1920s. Elegant colored tableware often attributed to other manufacturers.

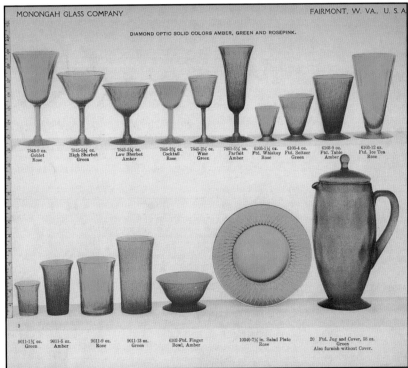

MONONGAH GLASS COMPANY   FAIRMONT, W. VA., U. S. A.

DIAMOND OPTIC SOLID COLORS AMBER, GREEN AND ROSEPINK.

7845-9 oz.   7845-5½ oz.   7845-5½ oz.   7845-2¾ oz.   7845-2½ oz.   7851-5½ oz.   6103-1½ oz.   6103-4 oz.   6103-9 oz.   6103-12 oz.
Goblet   High Sherbet   Low Sherbet   Cocktail   Wine   Parfait   Ftd. Whiskey   Ftd. Seltzer Ftd. Table   Ftd. Ice Tea
Rose   Green   Amber   Rose   Green   Amber   Rose   Green   Amber   Rose

9011-1¾ oz.   9011-5 oz.   9011-9 oz.   9011-13 oz.   6102-Ftd. Finger   10340-7½ in. Salad Plate   20 Ftd. Jug and Cover, 58 oz.
Green   Amber   Rose   Green   Bowl, Amber   Rose   Green
                                                                                                        Also furnish without Cover.

Monongah Glass colored catalog page circa 1920s. Elegant handmade tableware in amber, green, and rose pink with diamond optic.

Monongah Glass Co. Tall optic vase #0713 with crimped top pink, (found with Bo- Peep etch shown on original catalog page below, also possibly with other Monongah etchings) 9 ¼ inches, $20-24; sherbet line #6101 with distinctive two barrel stem, also shown below on original catalog page, pink, 4 ¾ inches, $18-24.

Monongah Glass Co. catalog page number 226 from an extensive circa 1920s catalog. Shown here is the decoration "Secretary's Primrose," Monongah's double plate etch #850.

Secretary's Primrose "deep plate etching double process," Monongah Glass Co. Tumbler, 4 ½ inches, $18-24; finger bowl, 2 ½ tall x 4 ¼ inches diameter, $22-26; pitcher with applied handle, 8 ½ inches, $85-95; sugar bowl, 3 inches tall, $30-35; creamer, 3 ½ inches, $30-35. All clear.

Left: This late 1920s catalog cover reflects the loss of local control of the Monongha Glass Co. as the company offices had moved to Indiana. The cover promotes a very dull, utilitarian tumbler.

Right: Monongha Glass tumbler images from a late 1920s catalog. If the cover of the catalog seemed dull, the interior is no more exciting.

NEEDLE ETCHING

This etching can be applied to any of our plain tumblers at slight cost. A distinctive decoration which will identify your concern.

Any lettering, gold band or enamel decoration desired can be supplied. This is a most economical and effective way to keep your name before the public.

Monongha Glass as late as the 1920s offered needle etched tumblers as shown by this catalog page illustration.

Roseland plate etching # 800, Monongah Glass Co. Pink saucer champagne/sherbet, 4 ½ inches, $30-36. Colored etched pieces of Monongah are uncommon.

Roseland plate etching #800, Monongah Glass Co. Individual almond, clear, 1 ¾ inches, $32-38; plate, clear, 7 inches, $12-16; straight sided sherbet, clear, 4 ¼ inches, $14-18.

Roseland plate etching #800, Monongah Glass Co. Handled ice tea or tumbler, clear, 5 ½ inches, $20-28; tumbler, optic, clear, 5 ½ inches, $18-24; finger bowl, 2 inches tall, 4 ½ inches diameter, $18-24; juice tumbler, 3 ½ inches, $14-20.

Roseland plate etching, Monongah Glass Co. All clear. Creamer, 3 ¼ inches, $28-34; sugar, 3 inches, $28-34; tall compote, 6 ½ inches tall x 6 inches diameter, $30-36; parfait, 7 inches, $18-24; goblet, 6 inches, $22-28.

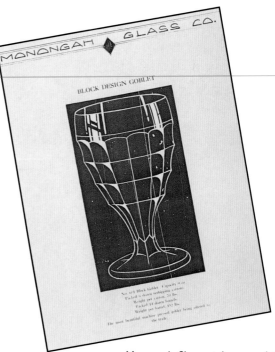

Monongah Glass catalog page, late 1920s; shown is a machine pressed "block design" goblet.

Monongah Glass. All clear. Secretary's Primrose double plate etching individual salt dip, 1 ½ inches tall x 1 ½ inches diameter, $26-32; Roseland plate etching parfait, 7 inches, $18-24; Roseland plate etching cordial, 4 inches, $28-38; Roseland plate etching individual almond dish, 1 ¾ inches tall x 2 ½ inches diameter, $20-28.

Monongah Glass catalog page circa 1920s with handmade elegant stemware lines.

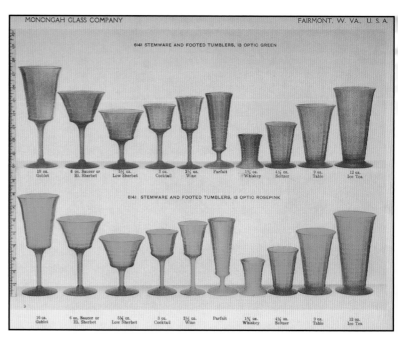

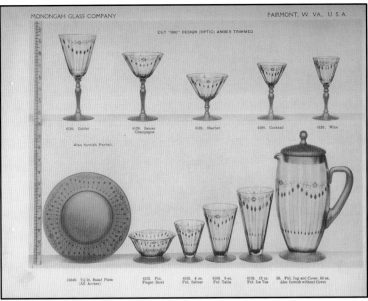

Monongha Glass colored catalog page circa 1920s.
Amber stem line #6120 with hand cut decoration and
tableware.

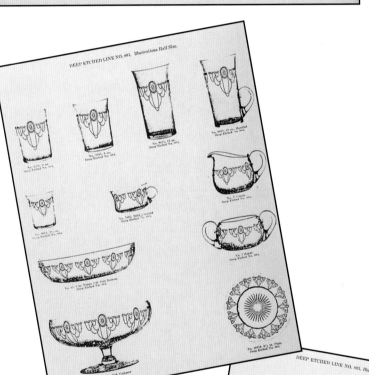

Monongah Glass Co. catalog page,
deep plate etching #803 shown in
abundance.

Monongah Glass catalog page circa 1920s showing the variety of
forms one decoration was available on. This deep plate etching #803 is
rarely attributed to Monongha.

Monongah Glass Co. catalog page, still
more deep plate etching #803.

Monongah Glass catalog page, circa 1920s, etched "Bo-Peep" design
#854 on stemware line #6102 and other forms. Bo-Peep is the most
recognized Monongah decoration. It is distinctive!

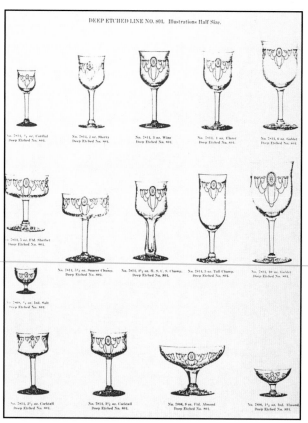

Monongah Glass Co. catalog page, deep plate etching
#803 continues.

Monongah Glass, circa 1920 catalog with stemware
line #6102 and deep plate etching #808.

Monongah Glass. Bo Peep double plate etching all pink. Footed tumbler, 4 ¾ inches, $55-65; iced tea, 6 inches,
$58-68; salad plate, 7 ½ inches, $45-54; twist stem sherbet/ saucer champagne, 5 ¾ inches, $45-55.

Jug, Monongah Glass. Roseland plate etching #800, hand applied handle, clear, 8 inches, $80-95.

Springtime plate etching, Monongah Glass Co. Sherbet, 4 ¼ inches, $18-24; wine, 4 ½ inches, $22-26; dessert plate, 7 inches, $18-22; handled ice tea or tumbler, 5 ½ inches, $24-28; tumbler, 4 inches, $20-24.

Twist stem #6102, Monongah Glass Co. Bo Peep plate etching, amber foot and stem, clear bowl, 5 ½ inches, $55-65. Goblet, optic, bowl amber with green stem and foot, 8 ¼ inches, $35-45.

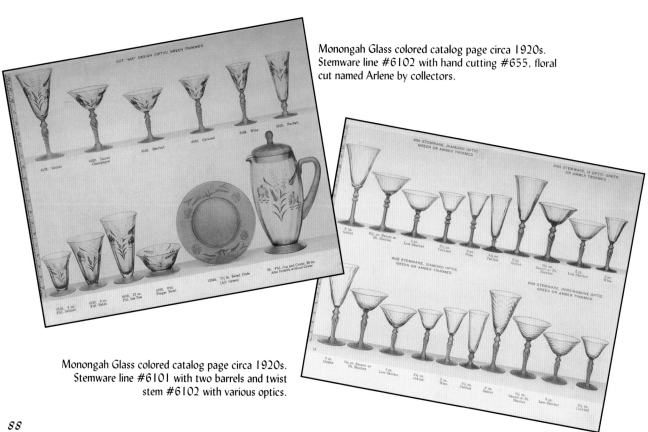

Monongah Glass colored catalog page circa 1920s. Stemware line #6102 with hand cutting #655, floral cut named Arlene by collectors.

Monongah Glass colored catalog page circa 1920s. Stemware line #6101 with two barrels and twist stem #6102 with various optics.

Morgantown Glassware Guild

Opening in Morgantown, West Virginia, in 1899 was Morgantown Glass Works. It was the second glass factory to open, following Seneca Glass, in a community that was to become known for glass.

This company operated under various names and management and would factually be known as Economy Tumbler Co. from 1903 until 1923, as Economy Glass Co. from 1924 until 1929, as Morgantown Glass Works from 1930 until 1937 and as Morgantown Glassware Guild from 1937 until 1975 when it closed. Amidst all this confusion, collectors have bundled together the products and history of this single factory and many companies into one story, calling it collectively Morgantown Glass. Morgantown is known for its diverse color production, for the offhand art glass, and for providing the formal state crystal to the White House under the Kennedy administration.

Two good guides to Morgantown Glass have been written and it is to those you should turn for details and specific information. The texts are:

Snyder, Jeffrey B. *Morgantown Glass: From Depression Glass Through the 1960s*. Atglen, Pennsylvania: Schiffer Publishing, 1998. 224 p.

Gallagher, Jerry. A *Handbook of Old Morgantown Glass*. Minneapolis, Minnesota: Privately published, 1995. 237 p.

El Patio, Morgantown Glass Works. 1930s products to match the casual Mexican motifs on dinnerware of the time. Cobalt foot with rings, clear bowl tumblers, 4 inches, $14-20; 5 inches, $16-22.

Golf Ball stem, Morgantown Glass Works. Goblet, clear foot and stem, peach optic bowl, 6 ¾ inches, $28-34; cordial, clear foot and stem, Stigel green bowl, 3 1/3 inches, $45-50; iced tea, clear foot and stem, ruby bowl, 6 ½ inches, $38-44; saucer champagne, clear foot and stem, ruby bowl, 4 inches, $34-40; azure blue foot, clear stem, azure optic bowl, 4 inches, $24-28.

No. 907 Morgantown Glass Works jade green 9 oz. tumblers, 3 ¾ inches, $28-38 each.

Advertisement for Morgantown Glass Works' El Patio line as it appeared in *China, Glass & Lamps* May 1936. Colors offered were tangerine, amber, blue, green, and in color and crystal combinations.

Jupiter vase, Morgantown Glass Works. Jade green, 5 ¼ inches, $280-300.

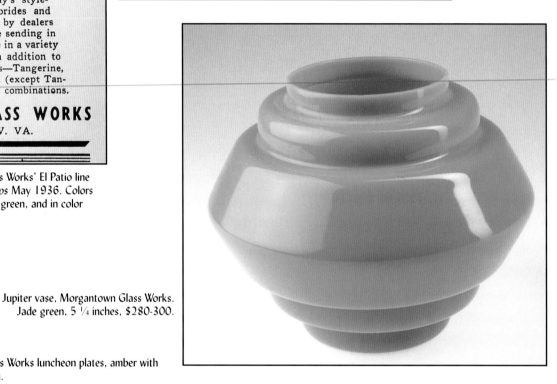

Two-tone Genova, Morgantown Glass Works luncheon plates, amber with blue edge, 8 ½ inches, $60-80 each.

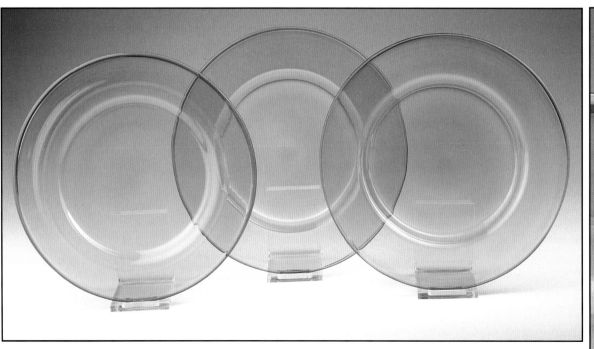

Fan Vase, Morgantown Glass Works. Cased amber over opal fan vase, 8 ½ inches tall, $400-600.

Morgantown Glass Works #546 jug and tumbler featured in *China, Glass & Lamps* July 1937. The jug was available in all crystal or with a body of blue, green, or ruby with a crystal handle. Color combinations like these were utilized by most handmade glass houses in the 1930s.

Electra vase, Morgantown Glass Works. Anna Rose drape optic body with Meadow green foot and reeded handles. *Courtesy Replacements, LTD.* $450-650.

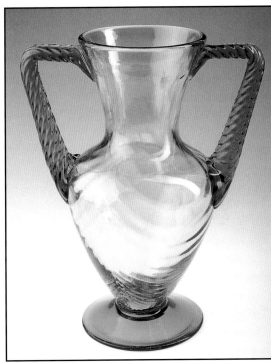

Genova two-tone plates, Morgantown Glass Works. Detailed close-up of applied glass trail of blue on amber plate. Made of thin crystal, these are confused with and attributed to Steuben and others.

7685—9-oz. Goblet—
Ruby bowl, Crystal base.

Autumn . . . colder days . . . increased entertaining . . . that's why weatherwise dealers are displaying Old Morgantown's famous Ruby Glass. The grand, warm color every hostess craves for her Hallowe'en, Thanksgiving or Christmas table. Ruby is offered in a wide variety of stemware designs, as well as lovely gift items. Our representatives cover the country—place your order now with your local Morgantown man.

MORGANTOWN GLASS WORKS
MORGANTOWN, W. VA.

Morgantown Glass Works advertisement, September 1936, shows a ruby stem line #7685. Whether the word Radiant was meant to be descriptive of the red glass the copy boasts of or to be a name for the line illustrated is unclear. Collectors have accepted this shape #7685 as Radiant.

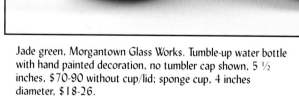

Virginia plate etching, Morgantown Glass Works. Tumbler, clear, 3 ¾ inches, $18-24; luncheon plate, 8 inches, $22-26.

Jade green, Morgantown Glass Works. Tumble-up water bottle with hand painted decoration, no tumbler cap shown, 5 ½ inches, $70-90 without cup/lid; sponge cup, 4 inches diameter, $18-26.

"Arena," Morgantown Glass Works. Enamel banded tumblers, ruby, 3 inches, $14-18; green, 4 ½ inches, $10-14.

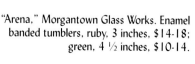

Richmond plate etching, Morgantown Glass Works. Saucer, clear, 6 inches, $4-8; tumbler, 5 inches, $ 12-16.

Mayfair plate etching, Morgantown Glass Works. Ice tea, clear, 5 ½ inches, $18-24; wine, clear, 5 ¾ inches, $12-16.

Morgantown Glass wedding vase, jade foot, black ball stem, flattened jade body, 9 ½ inches, $320-360. *West Virginia Museum of American Glass collection.*

Art Moderne stem, Morgantown Glass Co. Saucer champagne/sherbet, open stem, clear foot, black stem, clear bowl, lily pad hand cut gray and plate etch "Victoria Regina cut & etch decoration," 4 ¾ inches, $40-46; saucer champagne/ sherbet, azure blue, Sunrise Medallion plate etching, 6 ¼ inches, $32-38.

El Mexicano, Morgantown Glass Works. Seaweed color plate, 6 ½ inches, $24-32. Ice color shot glass, 2 ½ inches, $24-30. Seaweed color plate, 9 ¼ inches, $28-34. Ice color footed sherbet, 2 ½ inches, $16-24. Ice color plate, 7 ¾ inches, $26-32.

Sunrise Medallion, Morgantown Glass Works. Optic tumbler, 2 ½ inches, clear, $32-38; bud vase, pink, 10 ¼ inches, $160-180; clear plate, 6 inches, $18-24; wine, 5 inches, clear, $28-34.

Reverse twist stem, Morgantown Glass Works. Saucer champagne or sherbet, clear with unknown plate etching, 6 ¼ inches, $18-24. Clear foot and stem, cobalt blue bowl, double gold band decoration, $48-60.

Morgantown Glass Works. Marilyn plate etching sherbet, amber, 3 ¼ inches, $14-18; Bramble Rose plate etching, clear, optic, tumbler, 3 ½ inches, $14-18.

Fernlee plate etching, Morgantown Glass Works. Footed tumbler, clear, 4 ½ inches, $32-38.

Morgantown Glass Works. Sherbet, optic, bowl azure blue with unidentified gray cutting, 5 inches, $14-18.

Cased filament stems, Morgantown Glass Works. Spanish red filament saucer champagne, 5 ½ inches, $28-36; Carlton etch on #7606 1/2 Atehna line, black filament stem water goblet, $50-60.

Cased filament stems, Morgantown Glass Works. Black filament stem, Brilliant line saucer champagne with Carlton plate etching, 6 inches, circa 1931, $60-80; Spanish red filament wine, 4 ½ inches, $30-36.

Morgantown Glass Works. Yale stem wine, clear foot and stem, Stiegle green bowl, $80-95; wine, clear foot and stem, cobalt blue bowl, 5 ½ inches, $25-35.

Morgantown Glass Works 1936 ad for "Hollywood," a satin and platinum band and "lipstick red" decoration.

Morgantown Glass Works ad of June 1937 features a jug and tumbler in stacked rings. From Dunbar to Weston, Seneca to Cambridge, the glass houses of the 1930s were producing bold colored jugs with crystal handles and stacked ring patterns.

Rosamonde plate etching, Morgantown Glass Works. Brilliant line 7617, amber stem with clear bowl, goblet, 7 ½ inches, $34-42; parfait, 6 ½ inches, $28-36; footed tumbler, 8 inches, $18-26.

Ringed tumblers, Morgantown Glass Works. Tumbler with original blow pipe break off still intact, ruby, No Price established. Green tumbler showing finished product, 4 inches, $12-16.

Brilliant pattern, Morgantown Glass Works. All clear foot and stem ruby bowl sherbet/saucer champagne, 4 ¼ inches, $28-36; goblet, 7 inches, $42-48; cordial, 4 inches, $48-56; wine, 5 inches, $28-36.

New Martinsville Glass

New Martinsville Glass opened in 1900 and operated until 1944 when it changed it's name to Viking Glass. A report in the magazine *Retailing* 29 December 1941 reported the name change, but it was delayed due to World War II until the summer of 1944. It was stated the new firm would engage in "the manufacturer of hand-made, quality glassware of the heavy Swedish type." Thus the Viking name. In reality the products were not exclusively nor long styled after Swedish glass.

New Martinsville Glass produced pressed pattern glass and oil lamps in great numbers early in this century, echoing, if not emulating, the success of Riverside Glass in Wellsburg, West Virginia, a short distance up the Ohio River. It was at Riverside, a major lamp and pattern glass producer, that some of New Martinsville's leaders gained their glass skills. By the 1920s, the company was producing elegant and simple shapes in colors and with cuttings and decoration popular at the time: molasses cans, cake salvers, candle sticks, sandwich trays, and things as strictly practical as display vases for use in store displays! Items may included gray or light cutting as decoration when found.

The 1930s saw New Martinsville break away from simple and traditional. Novel small electric lamps were introduced, Vanity sets became a significant line and tableware patterns, such as the one today known as Moondrops, emerged in this period. The color offerings also broke loose. In 1932 we saw "the New Evergreen color" . . . a dark forest green, added to New Martinsville's existing colors of crystal, green, Ritz blue, amber, rose, ruby, and jade.

When in 1944 the Viking name was adopted, and later as the Second World War became a thing past, we see additions of "smart" new table settings and some of the heavy, crystal styles of European influence entering the New Martinsville offerings. The Swedish influence was long felt at Viking but the colorless, European look never dominated production. Color and whimsey remained. For a lengthy discussion of the history and products of New Martinsville Glass Company seek James Measell's book *New Martinsville Glass, 1900-1944.* Marietta, Ohio: Antique Publications, 1994.

New Martinsville Glass ad from *China, Glass & Lamps* 1925 shows a pressed oil lamp that easily could have been in style in 1890. Products like this often paid the bills in a glass house.

New Martinsville Glass was a major producer of dresser and vanity sets. This 1942 ad fills the void for European glass products no longer available due to the world war.

New Martinsville Glass 1933 ad featuring Moondrops, mentions their "new No. 37 Georgian line," a ringed pattern shown here, not the usual honeycomb styled Georgian pattern. Also new, the Evergreen color.

New Martinsville Glass 1936 ad for the #18/728 service.

Decanter and wine line #15, New Martinsville Glass. Ruby decanter with clear stopper. Shown in ads circa 1935. 9 ½ inches to the top of the decanter, $ 65-85; wine, ruby, 9 ½ inches, $16-22. Collection of Roy and Doris White.

"Addie" pattern No. 34, New Martinsville Glass. Footed tumbler, jade green, 4 ¾ inches, $24-30. Pattern #15 wine, cobalt blue, 4 ½ inches, $22-26. Pattern No. 34 "Addie" cup, cobalt blue, 2 ½ inches, $16-20.

Pattern No. 38, New Martinsville Glass. Tumblers, ruby, 3 ½ inches, $10-14; and decanter ruby with colorless stopper, 12 ½ inches, $65-72. Cocktail shaker with chrome lid, green, 9 ¾ inches, $60-70.

New Martinsville Glass ad from *The Pottery, Glass and Brass Salesman* January 1926. The smokers' set match book and the ad copy both show the NM monogram some circa 1920s New Martinsville glass will bear as an impressed mark.

Princess Bowl No. 10-12, New Martinsville Glass Co. Console bowl, blue with unattached black base. Both pieces bear "NM" monogram styled mark on bottom. Bowl with elegant gray cutting. Bowl, 12 inches diameter. Set $68-85.

New Martinsville Glass September 1925 ad for the "Chesterfield smokers' set, available in green or amber."

No. 723 Bridge Sugar and Cream Set

HERE'S ANOTHER great popular-price sales proposition. A right-up-to-the-minute individual sugar and cream set, on an appropriate basket tray with six-inch handle. The set is made of pot glass, pressed in specially designed moulds and nicely finished. Quantity lots to be had at a surprisingly low price.

Write us to-day—"strike the iron while it's hot."

New Martinsville Glass Mfg. Company
New Martinsville, W. Va.
Ira M. Clarke, General Manager
Frederick Skelton, 200 Fifth Avenue, New York representative

New Martinsville Glass ads from 1932. Top shows vanity set and a small bedroom lamp. Bottom image is of the "new" line #37, Moondrops. It was tumblers only at this point, available in crystal, green, Ritz blue, amber, rose, ruby, and jade.

New Martinsville Glass #723 Bridge sugar and cream set with basket-like tray.

Moondrops pattern No. 37, New Martinsville Glass. Compote, ruby, 3 ¾ inches tall, $38-42; ruby and chrome wine (two part, glass bowl with threaded base), 5 inches, $24-32.

Moondrops pattern No. 37, New Martinsville Glass. Three toed, three part divided relish, amber, 8 ¼ inches with chrome attached handle, $28-30.

101

Moondrops pattern No. 37, New Martinsville Glass. Low three toed bowl. Evergreen, 10 inches, $28-32.

Moondrops pattern decanters, New Martinsville Glass. Amber with clear stopper, 8 ¼ inches to top of decanter, $40-50; ruby with clear stopper, 7 ¼ inches to top of decanter, $65-80; green with clear stopper, 8 ¼ inches to top of decanter, $50-65. *West Virginia Museum of American Glass collection.*

FORT PITT HOTEL

Pittsburgh Show

ROOM 706

Jan. 8th to 16th

Introducing a new design idea in a liquor set. #37/4, decanter mounted on tripod on base; reproduced in detail in six glasses; comes in crystal, green, ritz blue, amber, rose, ruby and jade. But best of all will be its popular pricing.

Announcing A showing of a complete collection of interestingly new designs in well made merchandise, all styled to assure profitable promotion.

The

NEW MARTINSVILLE

GLASS MANUFACTURING CO.

IRA M. CLARKE, General Manager

NEW MARTINSVILLE
WEST VIRGINIA

CROCKERY AND GLASS JOURNAL for December, 1933   15

New Martinsville Glass ad of December 1933 introducing #37/4, the so called rocket decanter in the Moondrops line.

Moondrops pattern No. 37, New Martinsville Glass. Individual sugar, green, 2 ¾ inches, $14-20; individual sugar, ruby, 2 ¾ inches, $16-24; and individual creamer, ruby, 3 inches, $16-24.

Moondrops pattern No. 37, New Martinsville Glass. Coffee cup, amber, 2 ½ inches tall, $8-12; candlestick, Evergreen, 4 ¾ inches tall, $16-20; and tab handled, amethyst, three toed server, 1 ¾ inches tall, $18-22.

Moondrops pattern No. 37, New Martinsville Glass. Light green handled tumbler/mug, 5 inches, $24-30. European tumbler, smokey green with hand applied prunts on which the "moondrops" of New Martinsville were modeled. 6 inches. No value established.

Moondrops pattern No. 37, New Martinsville Glass. Evergreen handled small mug (shot glass), 2 ¾ inches, $18-22. European tumbler, smokey green with hand applied prunts or moondrops, 3 inches. Note that far from claiming a new design, 1933 ads introducing Moondrops said it was "reminiscent of the age of chivalry." These Germanic styled, handmade glass forms with prunts or applied designs of glass to help maintain a grip on the vessel seem the likely source, if not the exact prototypes, for the "age of chivalry" designs.

New Martinsville Glass ad of 1936 with an all over etching identified as #25.

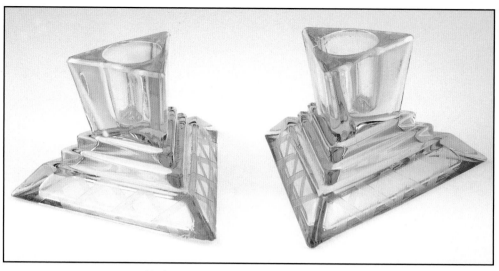

Modernistic pattern No. 33, New Martinsville Glass. Candlesticks with gray cuttings on base, "depression green," 2 ¼ inches tall, pair $60-70.

Modernistic pattern No. 33, New Martinsville Glass. Three sided vase, black, 8 ½ inches, $80-100; creamer with enamel decoration, black, 2 ¾ inches, $36-44.

New Martinsville Glass Co. is adapting the Viking glass name in this transitional *House and Garden* ad of May 1944. The products shown are the figural seals, part of the highly collectible animal line made by New Martinsville - Vikings.

Janice pattern, New Martinsville Glass. Creamer, 4 inches, $12-16; and sugar, 3 ¼ inches, $12-16; cruet with stopper, 4 ¾ inches, $24-30; all light blue.

Janice pattern, New Martinsville Glass. Footed sherbet, ruby, 2 ¼ inches, $12-16; shaker, clear with metal cap, 3 inches, $6-8.

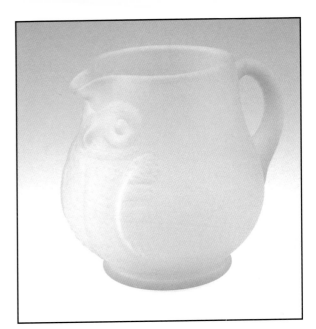

Owl Jug, New Martinsville Glass, design patent 76,409 filed 31 January, 1928, clear frosted, 4 inches, $38-42.

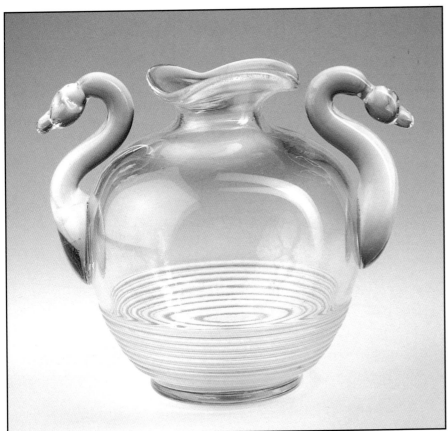

"Swan Janice," New Martinsville Glass. Vase with hand applied swan handles, factory number "111-2 SJ," clear, 4 ½ inches, $30-40.

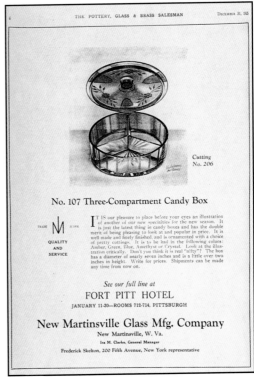

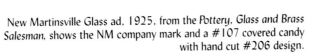

New Martinsville Glass ad, 1925, from the Pottery, Glass and Brass Salesman, shows the NM company mark and a #107 covered candy with hand cut #206 design.

Crystal Eagle pattern No. 18, New Martinsville Glass. Ash tray (similar to powder box bottom with cigarette rests added), amber, 5 ¼ inches, $12-16; two light candlestick, amber, 5 ½ inches tall, $28-36.

Radiance pattern, New Martinsville Glass. Punch cup, light blue, 2 ½ inches, $8-12; small stemmed server, unknown etch, clear, 5 ½ inches diameter, $16-20; creamer with unknown etch, clear, 3 ¼ inches tall, $10-14.

New for 1937---

RADIANCE

AN unusual design in table glassware, radiant with highlights and glitter. Appealing to the discriminating, but not radical. "Radiance" is the glassware every buyer will want to see. Com. !

During Pittsburgh Exhibit

ROOM 690

Hotel William Penn

January 11 to 20

Each piece of "Radiance" glassware is decorative in tone, but it will also take decoration. For the shape, we have developed a new etched design, "Meadow-wreath". See it and marvel!

In addition to tableware pieces, the new line will include Vases, Console Sets, Candelabra, Relishes and other occasional items. Luncheon set composition, too.

"Radiance" will be priced popularly.

THE NEW MARTINSVILLE GLASS MFG. CO.

NEW MARTINSVILLE, W. VA.

New Martinsville Glass December 1936 ad proclaims New Radiance . . . and an unusual design in tableware.

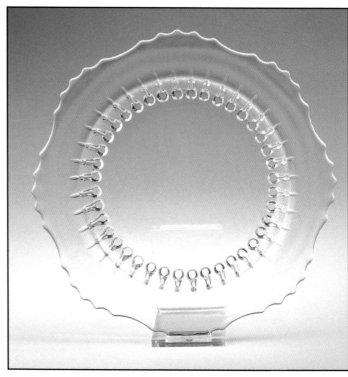

Radiance pattern, New Martinsville Glass. Luncheon plate, clear, 8 ¼ inches, $8-12.

Radiance pattern, New Martinsville Glass. Pair oil and vinegar bottles/cruets, amber with clear stoppers, 6 inches, $28-38 each.

Radiance pattern, New Martinsville Glass. Flared bowl, unknown etch, clear, 13 inches, $32-38.

214/7164—15 Piece Luncheon Set. Ruby red glass in "Radiance" pattern, scalloped edge. Four 8½ inch salad plates, four cups, four saucers, sugar, creamer and cake or sandwich plate, diameter 14 inches. (Matches 214/7177 Salad Set, 214/7178 Console Set and 214/7176 Assortment of Bowls) 1 set in carton. ....Per set $10.00

New Martinsville Glass Radiance pattern featured in Butler Bros. Wholesale catalog of the late 1930s.

Ruby, New Martinsville Glass. Moondrops pattern No. 37 three toed ash tray, ruby, 6 inches, $26-30; Janice luncheon plate, ruby, 8 ½ inches, $22-26; Moondrops pattern No. 37 handled tumbler/mug, ruby, 5 inches, $34-38.

Paden City

Paden City, West Virginia, is today the home of two glass factories, one manufacturing glass marbles and one producing colored sheet art glass by the casting process. Glass has been made in this small town along the Ohio River since Empire Glass Co. opened here in 1903 or '04. Empire has been in continuous business and is today Paul Wismach Glass Co. Inc, the flat glass producers mentioned above whose glass was used by Tiffany in manufacturing lamp shades. The town, like many neighboring towns, has a rich glass history.

In 1916 the Paden City Glass Manufacturing Company opened. It was an immediate success. The beginning investment by stockholders had been $100,000. Success was so prompt that within one year the investors had been paid off! Hand blown and hand pressed wares were made, largely for other companies to market or decorate. Later in house decorating was very successful. In 1924 the etching and decorating department proved so successful that it was expanded and new equipment added to met demands.

In 1930 Paden City Glass listed their manufacturing ability to be one fourteen pot furnace, two continuous tanks with eleven rings and two day tanks. *China, Glass and Lamps* for March 1932 reported "the new ruby etched glassware of Paden City Glass Mfg. Co. is creating a wave of favorable comment . . . the trellis etching in non-tarnishing silver on ruby is proving a good seller. The new etched ruby comes in wine sets, cocktail sets, and table pieces." In September of 1932 the same trade journal featured an ad showing a cocktail mixer, tray, and glasses in milk or opal glass "in a variety of . . . decorations to stimulate Fall and Holiday selling." Specifically mentioned was a Snowflake line(?).

One of the popular lines produced by Paden City was their Line 555. An interesting note appears in the archives at Fenton Art Glass written in hand by J. R. (Raymond) Price, long associated with the National Association of Manufacturers of Pressed and Blown Glassware. Mr. Price served as a liaison between friendly but often competing companies in the glass industry. This note reads, "#555 line was originated by George Daner, Sr. About 1940-41. Originally this line had a full beaded edge. When the new mould was put into operation I called Mr. Daner [about] the similarity of the #555 to Imperials 'Candlewick' and after some discussion it was decided to add the 'tail' to each bead – making a sort of tear drop edge."

Paden City colors had creative names and great variety. They included: opal or milk glass; black; mulberry (their name for amethyst); Cheriglo (their pink); yellow; dark green; crystal; red; amber; cobalt blue; light blue; rose (a darker pink); and a unique green called by employees apple green.

As progress seemed inevitable, Paden City Glass purchased the fully automated American Glass Company, also in Paden City, to aid them in price competitiveness. The new plant proved to be a great financial burden and the Board of Directors closed the company 21 September 1951.

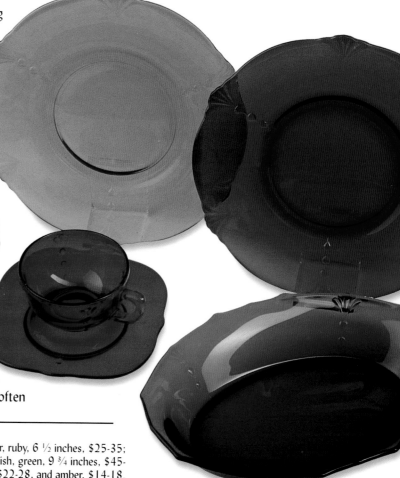

Crows Foot, Paden City Glass Co. Cup, 2 inches, and saucer, ruby, 6 ½ inches, $25-35; stemmed cheese dish/compote, amber, $18-24; oval vegetable dish, green, 9 ¾ inches, $45-50; luncheon plates, 9 ¼ inches, blue, $22-28, and amber, $14-18.

Crows Foot Bowl, Paden City Glass Co. Orchid plate etching, clear, 13 inches, $45-65.

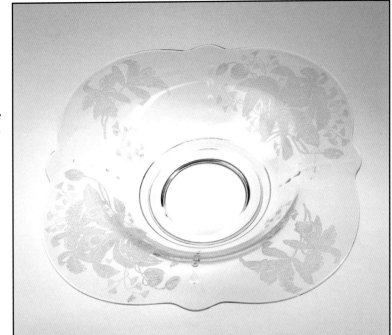

Bowl, Paden City Glass Co. Three toed bowl, xx line plate etch garden scene, clear, 11 ½ inches, $30-45; Crows Foot single light candlestick, amber, same etch, $40-48.

Compote, Paden City Glass Co. Leeowen plate etching, amber, $60-80, and undecorated cobalt blue, $45-60. Both 6 ¾ inches.

Tumblers, Paden City Glass Co. Gazebo plate etching, $12-18, and Flower Basket plate etching, $8-14, both 3 ¼ inches.

Ardith plate etching, Paden City Glass Co. All clear. Bar bottle, 10 ½ inches, $30-40; compote, 3 ¾ inches, $28-36; single light candlestick, gold trim, 6 ¼ inches, $32-35.

Paden City Glass Line 300 was "new" in this *China, Glass & Lamps* ad of December 1928.

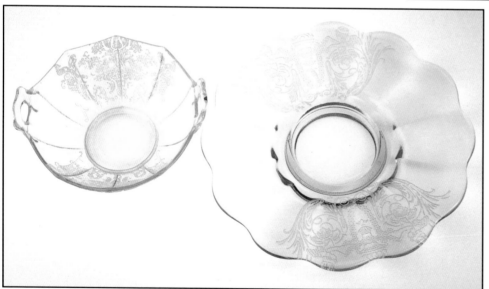

Paden City Glass Co. Two open handles, topaz bowl, Gothic Garden plate etching, 2 1/8 inches, $28-36; plate, Line #300 with Cupid plate etching, green, 8 inches, $25-35.

Paden City Glass Co. creamer, light blue, 3 ½ inches, $18-22; sugar with Frost plate etching, clear, 3 inches, $16-20.

Paden City Glass Co. #2000 Mystic line, tab handled oval console bowl, clear, 12 ½ inches, $20-28.

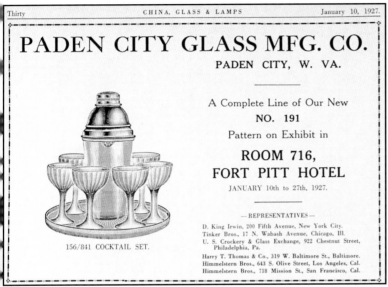

Paden City Glass Co. January 1927 *China, Glass & Lamps* ad shows line 191 cocktail shaker and glasses.

Candlestick, Paden City Glass Co. Two light with unknown gray hand cutting, clear, 5 ¾ tall x 8 ¼ inches wide, $35-48.

Party Line #210, Paden City Glass Co. All amber. Creamer, 3 ¼ inches, $10-14; Cocktail shaker shown with no lid, 7 ½ inches, $55-65 with lid; sherbet, 3 ¼ inches, $6-8; goblet, 6 ¼ inches, $12-14; footed tumbler, 3 ¾ inches, $10-14.

Paden City Glass December 1925 ad for #80 smokers set.

Vase, Paden City Glass. Panel optic vase with floral etch, green, 10 inches, $180-225.

Paden City Glass ad from 1935 shows the #175 three piece "Fleur De Lis" console set available in crystal, amber, green, royal blue, and ruby.

Soda fountain ware Line 210, Paden City Co. Malt glass, green, 7 inches, $14-18; sherbet, green, 3 inches, $6-8; saucer with "Associated Gas and Electric System" plate etched seal on rim, green, 5 3/4 inches, $4-6; footed tumbler, red, 3 1/2 inches, $18-20; soda glass, clear, 5 inches, $3-5.

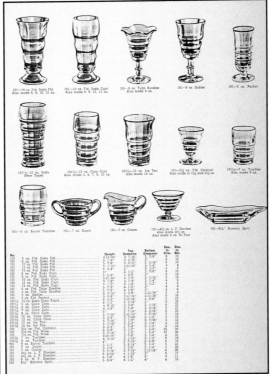

Paden City Glass catalog page showing Line 191 and 191 ½ circa 1930s.

Paden City Glass catalog page showing Line 191 and 191 ½ circa 1930s.

Jug with lid, Paden City Glass Co. Harvester plate etching, amber, 6 ¾ inch, $100-120.

Decanters Paden City Glass Co. Footed wine with plate etching Spring Orchard, 4 inches, $14-20; decanter with stopper, etched "GIN" and Spring Orchard etch 7 ¼ inches to top of decanter, $55-68; decanter with stopper, plate etch "Eleanor" and gold wash decoration, 7 ¼ inches to top of decanter, $60-75.

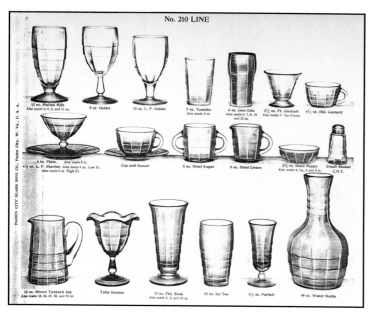

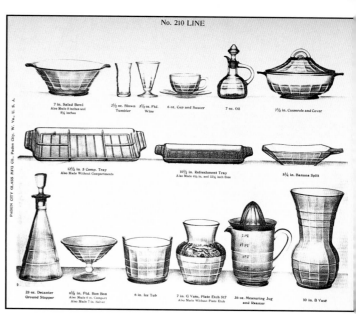

Paden City Glass Co. undated catalog No. 210 Line.

Paden City Glass Co. undated catalog No. 210 Line.

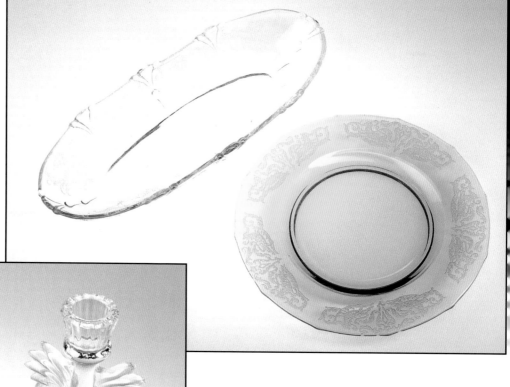

Leeuwen Plate Etching, Paden City Glass Co. Celery, clear, 11 ½ inches, $40-60; luncheon plate, amber, 8 ¼ inches, $28-35.

Candlesticks, Paden City Glass Co. #215 Glades candlestick, Frost plate etch, clear, 6 ½ inches, $35-42; Gazebo plate etching (Maya shape?), gold encrusted, clear, 6 ¼ inches, $45-55.

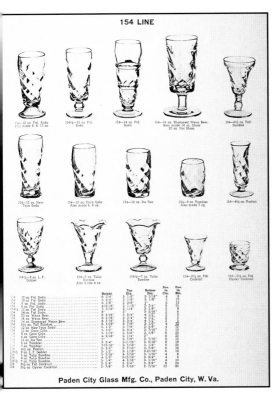

154 LINE

Paden City Glass Mfg. Co., Paden City, W. Va.

154 LINE

Paden City Glass Mfg. Co., Paden City, W. Va.

Paden City Glass Co. undated catalog Line #154.

Paden City Glass Co. undated catalog Line #154.

Comet pattern Line #777, Paden City Glass Co. Creamer, 3 ½ inches, $18-24; mayonnaise bowl, 2 ¼ inches deep x 4 ½ inches, $2-24 (*$22-24?); sugar, 3 ¼ inches, $18-24.

Comet pattern Line # 777, Paden City Glass Co. Center handled server, blue, 11 inches, $40-50.

Comet pattern Line #777 Candlestick, Paden City Glass Co. Single light, Aster plate etch, clear, 4 ½ inches, $20-30.

Paden City Glass Co. January 1933 *China, Glass & Lamps* ad for Line #881 "Wotta" tableware available in crystal, green, cheriglo, amber, royal blue, topaz, and ruby.

Paden City Glass Co. 1932 ad for Snow Flake, new creation in color, "beautiful white."

Paden City Glass Co. 1936 *China, Glass & Lamps* ad featuring #211 Vanity set.

Creamers, Paden City Glass Co. Meadow Bloom plate etch, clear creamer, 3 ½ inches, $14-22; Pam's Floral plate etching on line # 555 creamer, 3 ½ inches, $16-22.

Crows Foot pattern, Paden City Glass Co. Cream and sugar, milk glass, 2 ¾ to top of handles, $20-24 each.

Paden City clear Crows Foot blank, unknown peacock etch, 2 ¾ inches to top of handle, $40-45 each. Note: there is a "flock" of varying peacock-themed Paden City plate etchings and I find them confusing.

Crows Foot pattern, Paden City Glass. Orchid plate etching on three panels and "Patrol 19 (elf-like character) 33" on fourth side, 11 ½ inches. *Museum purchase, made possible in part by gift of Kelly O'Kane. $300-400. West Virginia Museum of American Glass collection.*

Crows Foot, Paden City Glass Co. Bowl, two open tab handles, black, 3 ¼ inches tall, 11 ¾ inches at handles, $100-120; Compote, topaz, 3 ¾ inches, $22-26.

Gazebo plate etching, Paden City Glass Co. Center handled server line #555 with gold encrusted Gazebo plate etching, clear, 11 inches diameter, $45-52.

Plate, Paden City Glass Co. Plate with Basket Flower plate etching, line #555, clear, 11 inches, $24-28.

No. 555 Line

12 in. Console Bowl No. 2 shape. - P. E. Baby Orchid

2-way Candlestick. P. E. Baby Orchid

2-way Candlestick. P. E. Baby Orchid

7 in. 3-Part Candy Box and Cover.
Cut No. 86

11 in. Handled Sandwich Tray
Cut No. 533

11 in. 2-Handle Salad Bowl
P. E. Baby Orchid

12 in. Covered Cheese and Cracker.
Cut No. 535

13 in. 2 Handle Plate - P. E. Baby Orchid

7 in. High-Foot Bowl and Cover.
Cut No. 535

11 in. Plate. Cut No. 86

Sugar and Cream Set. Cut No. 86

10 in. 3-Part Relish. Cut No. 533

3-Piece Mayonnaise Set - P. E. Lady Orchid

Paden City Glass Co., Paden City, W. Va.

Paden City Glass Co. undated catalog page showing
Line #555 with various cuttings and etchings.

Gazebo plate etching, Paden City Glass Co. Swan handled with gold
encrusted Gazebo etching, clear, 10 ½ inches, $60-75.

Paden City Glass Co. January 1932 ad introducing
Line #991 in crystal, green, cheriglo, amber, ruby,
and royal blue.

119

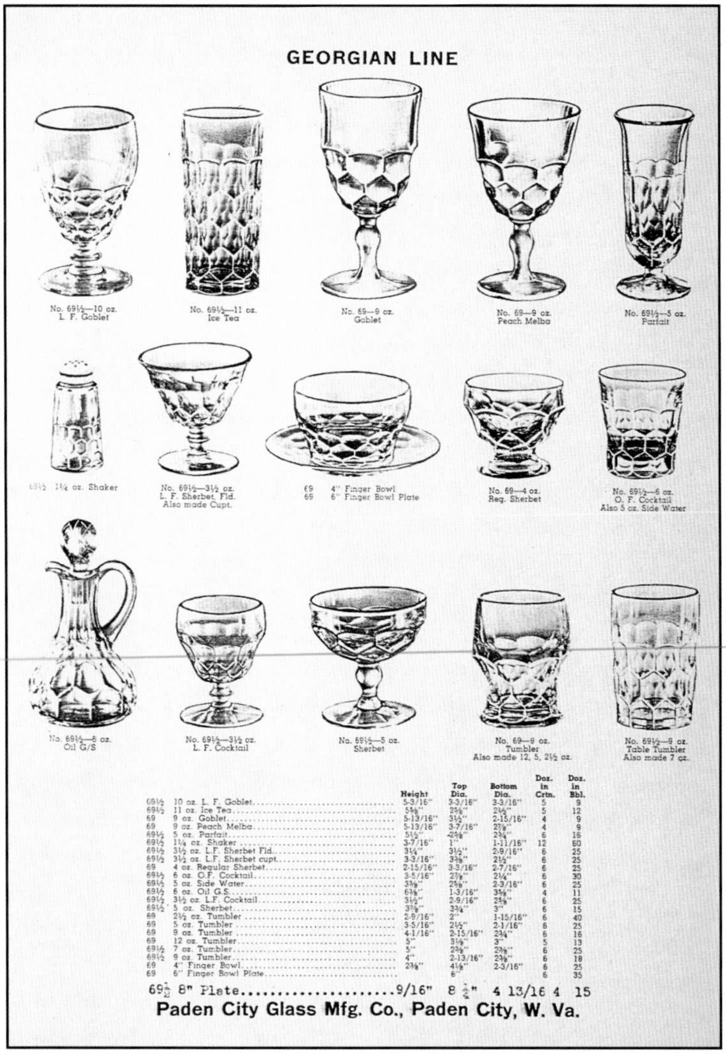

GEORGIAN LINE

No. 69½—10 oz.
L. F. Goblet

No. 69½—11 oz.
Ice Tea

No. 69—9 oz.
Goblet

No. 69—9 oz.
Peach Melba

No. 69½—5 oz.
Parfait

69½ 1¼ oz. Shaker

No. 69½—3½ oz.
L. F. Sherbet, Fld.
Also made Cupt.

69 4" Finger Bowl
69 6" Finger Bowl Plate

No. 69—4 oz.
Reg. Sherbet

No. 69½—6 oz.
O. F. Cocktail
Also 5 oz. Side Water

No. 69½—6 oz.
Oil G/S

No. 69½—3½ oz.
L. F. Cocktail

No. 69½—5 oz.
Sherbet

No. 69—9 oz.
Tumbler
Also made 12, 5, 2½ oz.

No. 69½—9 oz.
Table Tumbler
Also made 7 oz.

		Height	Top Dia.	Bottom Dia.	Doz. in Crtn.	Doz. in Bbl.
69½	10 oz. L. F. Goblet	5-3/16"	3-3/16"	3-3/16"	5	9
69½	11 oz. Ice Tea	5⅝"	2⅝"	2½"	5	12
69	9 oz. Goblet	5-13/16"	3½"	2-15/16"	4	9
69	9 oz. Peach Melba	5-13/16"	3-7/16"	2⅞"	4	9
69½	5 oz. Parfait	5½"	2⅝"	2¾"	6	16
69½	1¼ oz. Shaker	3-7/16"	1"	1-11/16"	12	60
69½	3½ oz. L.F. Sherbet Fld.	3¼"	3½"	2-9/16"	6	25
69½	3½ oz. L.F. Sherbet cupt.	3-3/16"	3⅜"	2½"	6	25
69	4 oz. Regular Sherbet	2-15/16"	3-3/16"	2-7/16"	6	25
69½	6 oz. O.F. Cocktail	3-5/16"	2⅞"	2¼"	6	30
69½	5 oz. Side Water	3⅜"	2⅝"	2-3/16"	6	25
69½	6 oz. Oil G.S.	6⅜"	1-3/16"	3⅝"	4	11
69½	3½ oz. L.F. Cocktail	3½"	2-9/16"	2⅝"	6	25
69½	5 oz. Sherbet	3⅞"	3¾"	3"	6	15
69	2½ oz. Tumbler	2-9/16"	2"	1-15/16"	6	40
69	5 oz. Tumbler	3-5/16"	2½"	2-1/16"	6	25
69	9 oz. Tumbler	4-1/16"	2-15/16"	2¾"	6	16
69	12 oz. Tumbler	5"	3⅛"	3"	5	13
69½	7 oz. Tumbler	5"	2⅜"	2⅜"	6	25
69½	9 oz. Tumbler	4"	2-13/16"	2⅜"	6	18
69	4" Finger Bowl	2⅜"	4⅛"	2-3/16"	6	25
69	6" Finger Bowl Plate		6"		6	35
69½	8" Plate	9/16"	8 ½"	4 13/16	4	15

Paden City Glass Mfg. Co., Paden City, W. Va.

Paden City Glass Co. original undated catalog page for the "Georgian line #69 and 69 ½."

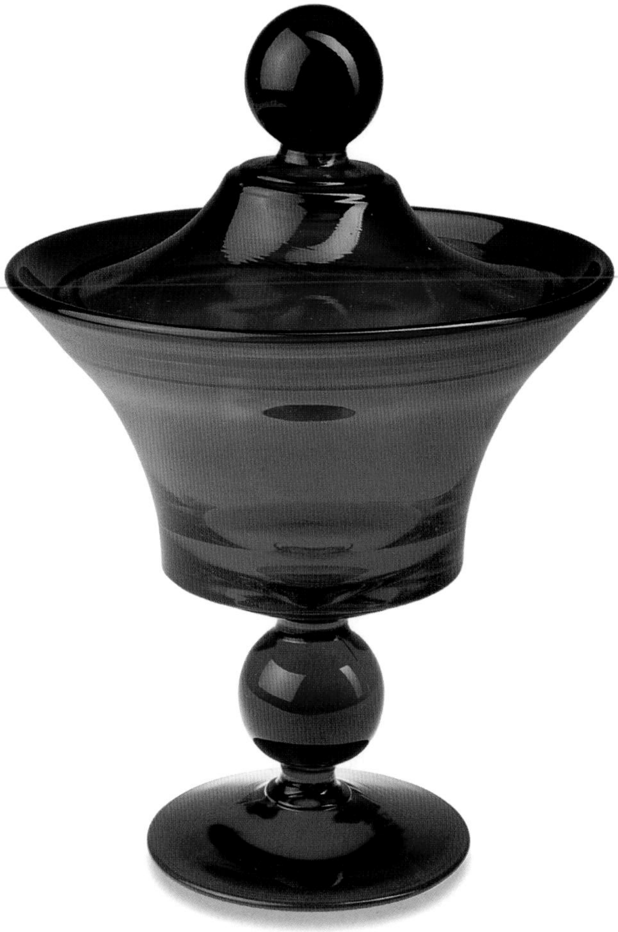

Paden City Glass covered candy, ruby, 7 inches to top of base, $50-65. *Roy and Doris White collection.*

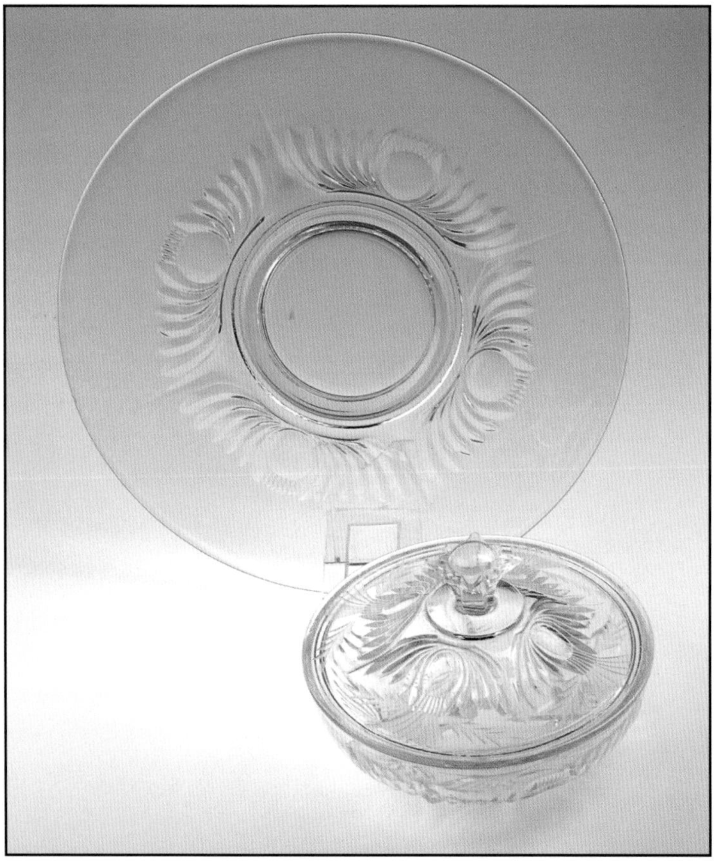

Mayan pattern, Paden City Glass Co. Under plate, blue, 12 ¼ inches, $20-24; covered three part divided candy with unknown gray hand cutting, 7 inches in diameter.

Paramount Glass

Glass production in this town along the Ohio River is little known today but millions of marbles, children's glass dishes, light bulbs, and other products have come from a series of lesser known factories here (see Alley story earlier in this volume). Paramount Glass is really a tale of two cities. Stanislaus Kizinski is the common thread in following Paramount Glass. He learned his trade as a youth in Poland before migrating to America. With his brothers he owned a successful factory in Szydlowiec that was built around 1906. Stanislaus migrated in 1909 and found work in Swissvale, Pennsylvania, with Nicholas Kopp.

In 1912 Louis Kanfield founded the Star City Glass Company near Morgantown, West Virginia, and Kizinski relocated there. Beside the glass house were abandoned lumber yards and Kizinski, with friends Ladislaus Kozlowski and Louis Wojciechowski, whom he had grown up with back in Poland, purchased the property. Immediately after World War I, a glass factory was built on this site. Due to several factors, it shortly failed but a local baker had faith in Kizinski and helped in his purchasing and placing in operation Paramount Glass Co. in 1921. The factory was prosperous until destroyed by fire in 1928. Rebuilding would have been costly. A then vacant factory

in St. Mary's, West Virginia, was purchased by Kizinski and Paramount Glass relocated.

Paramount produced crystal blanks for decorating shops who cut, etched, and applied silver and gold decorations. Additionally Kazinski was known for his glass chemistry and ability to create glass batches of exceptional color. Paramount produced rose, cobalt blue, amethyst, and emerald green. A 1903 letter notes that Paramount was making iron mould jugs (pitchers), blown plain and with optics. In 1935 Paramount is listed in the *Glass Factory Yearbook* as having six day tanks with twelve rings for production. The product lines are detailed as being plain and colored tumblers, stemware, tableware, and specialties.

In the summer of 1943 another fire, always the bane of glass houses, ended the production of Paramount. Paramount produced glass in St. Mary's for fifteen years.

Stanislaus Kizinski worked at Fenton Art Glass later in life and died in 1961. Amidst the great ravages that have swept across Poland, the factory he helped design and build in 1905 was still producing around 1980 and may be active yet today, a testimonial to a man and his family's love of the glass industry.

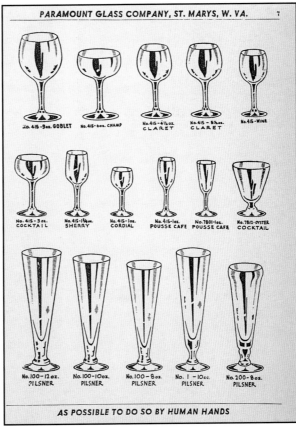

Left: Cover to an undated Paramount Glass Co catalog.

Right: Paramount Glass undated catalog, page shows ringed cocktail, finger bowl, and other objects that are distinctive enough to be identified as Paramount.

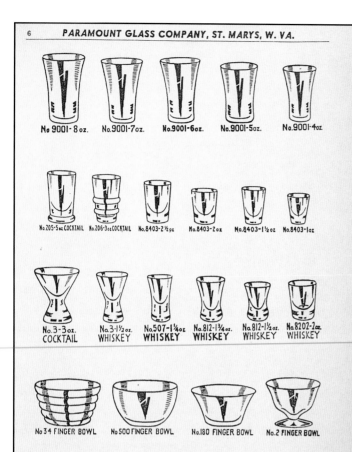

No. 9001- 8 oz.   No.9001-7oz.   No.9001-6oz.   No.9001-5oz.   No.9001-4oz.

No.205-5oz COCKTAIL   No.206-3oz COCKTAIL   No.8403-2½oz   No.8403-2oz   No.8403-1½oz   No.8403-1oz

No.3-3oz. COCKTAIL   No.3-1½oz. WHISKEY   No.507-1¼oz WHISKEY   No.812-1¾oz WHISKEY   No.812-1½oz WHISKEY   No.8202-2oz WHISKEY

No.34 FINGER BOWL   No.500 FINGER BOWL   No.180 FINGER BOWL   No.2 FINGER BOWL

ALL ITEMS MADE AS NEAR ACTUAL CAPACITY

Paramount Glass undated catalog, page showing handmade stemware that could be distinguished only by color. See text.

Paramount Glass undated trade journal ad page describing the company's goblets.

Goblets

ARE GOOD

and here you find variety

Shapes

Sizes

Styles

Colored stemware brilliant and properly proportioned. Two-tone styles with crystal feet. *And the newest low foot luncheon goblet.* Delicate tones in the new virgin green and blush-pink rose. Then the bright colors of ritz blue, smoke amber and amethyst are moving very well. You should have a complete display of these.

PARAMOUNT GLASS CO.

ST. MARYS, W. Va.

Seneca Glass Co.

Seneca Glass has its origins in the same factory in Fostoria, Ohio, where Fostoria Glass began. Fostoria opened there in 1891 and had moved to Moundsville, West Virginia, at the end of 1891, leaving behind an empty glass house. Seneca was organized and immediately occupied the then vacant Fostoria factory, only to relocate itself to West Virginia in 1896. From 1896 until 1983, Seneca operated from a sprawling factory in Morgantown, West Virginia, along the railroad and Monongahela River. Noteworthy is that Seneca was the first glass factory to this community that would become home to some twenty plus hot glass producers in the century to follow. Immediately adjacent to Seneca Glass was Old Morgantown (earlier known as Economy Tumbler), Beaumont Glass, Jones Window Glass, and Dura Glass (operating under several names in a short period of a few years). This concentration of glass houses employed hundreds and hundreds of glass workers. It was a stretch of continuous glass factories creating an uncommon if not unique glass community of thousands dependent on the industry.

Seneca's story begins with a number of German glass workers originally from the Black Forest area of Germany relocating to Ohio to work for themselves. The first company president was Otto Jeager (see Bonita Glass in this volume). Early Seneca must have been successful with relocation to West Virginia beginning a period of amazing growth and acclaim.

From the earliest years Seneca was recognized for quality. In 1898, a local lad wrote back to his hometown paper of seeing cut glass in a Nova Scotia, Canada, china store that took his fancy and was surprised to learn it was from "back home" in Morgantown. Seneca Glass was used in the White House by the McKinleys and later used by then Vice President Lyndon Johnson. Seneca has a long and successful story.

In the time of our focus Seneca, a glass house known for colorless and fine cut lead glass, became engaged in making a range of colored glass, something it is little known for today.

A 1931 Seneca catalog has survived and the use of cobalt blue glass with etched designs and rims and often with heavy platinum encrustations were the rage. It was a diverse catalog with offerings of candlesticks, console bowls, stem lines, compotes, vases, and more.

By 1936 Seneca was producing tumblers in color for casual use. Its design patented No. D 60637 Streamline Tumblers were offered in "burgundy, Amberina, azure blue, Florentine green, cobalt blue, and crystal." (CG&L: May 1936)

In 1936, when Pope Gosser China Company introduced their quickly successful tableware line Candlewick. It was a crystal line by Seneca, not the later popularized Imperial Glass line by the same name, that was co-marketed with the Candlewick china.

Seneca Candlewick was offered in "all crystal, or crystal with colored bases of Ruby, green, amber or cobalt blue." (C&GJ: November 1936) An acid etched pattern adorns the bowl exactly like the Pope Gosser china design, both reminiscent of the early American needle craft of candlewick.

As if quality glass were immune to depression, Seneca offered in the 1930s two new patterns of "superbly executed" stemware lines. One featured an Oriental butterfly and lotus motif and was called Manchu, the other had a rose and bird pattern and was called Westminster. The stems included the difficult to manufacture air trap bubble, with three faceted bulges in the long stem. In 1937 these "patterns can be retailed for $150." By the dozen or per stem, that was an amazing amount in the 1930s and this text suggests that is per stem!? (CG&L October 1937) The same year saw Seneca running illustrated ads for large cut punch bowls, cut ladles, and cut cups, all in the same pattern. Seneca had representatives with permanent show rooms in seven major cities by 1937.

In 1939, Seneca continued the color offerings as ads noted a new line that "can be had in all crystal or in crystal bowl and foot with blue, amber, green, amethyst, or ocean blue ball stem." Remember, Seneca is not commonly know as a colored glass producer!

The year 1940 saw Seneca tumblers looking entirely unlike the earlier Streamlined ones. A new corset shaped, or "pinched," line was being made and billed as an answer to the demand for Early American glassware. Advertisements note they were available in eight colors or crystal!

By 1942, a writer for *China and Glass* visited Seneca and wrote "a few years ago when there was such a craze for color, Seneca put out some exceptionally good-looking tones. One of the best selling was its amber color, which it called 'Amberina'. Others were Wild Rose and Emerald Green. Now of course—as I hardly need tell you—there is little color on the market, but Seneca has a nice Cranberry and several different stemware shapes with Cranberry bowls and crystal stems and feet." (November 1942)

Seneca continued to produce some of America's finest quality lead cut glass until its closing in 1983.

For additional details on the elegant cuttings of Seneca Glass see:

Page, Bob and Dale Frederiksen. *Seneca Glass Company 1891-1983: A Stemware Identification Guide*. Greensboro, North Carolina: Page-Frederiksen Publishing Co., 1995.

Seneca Glass Co. undated circa 1910s catalog
page. Deep plate etch #609 "Rose" design.

Seneca Glass Co. undated circa 1910s catalog page.
Deep plate etch #609 "Rose" design.

Seneca Glass Co. undated circa 1910s catalog page.
Deep plate etch #600 "Scroll" design.

Seneca Glass Co. undated circa 1910s catalog
page. Deep plate etch #600 "Scroll" design.

Seneca Glass Co. undated circa 1910s catalog page. Deep plate etch #608 "Grape" design. Remember every glass house almost had a grape plate etch and they are often similar.

Seneca Glass Co. undated circa 1910s catalog page. Deep plate etch #610 "Pansy" design.

Briar Rose plate etching, Seneca Glass Co. Creamer, 3 inches, $22-26; cruet, no stopper, 4 ½ inches, $45-55 with stopped; candy with optic, no lid, 6 ½ inches, 40-48 with lid; compote, 3 inches tall x 4 ½ inches diameter, $30-40. All clear.

Rose plate etching #609, Seneca Glass Co. Mustard pot, missing lid, clear, 2 ½ inches, $30-38 with lid; handled ice tea, clear, 5 inches, $28-34.

Seneca Glass Co. pitched their "patented" streamline tumblers in this June 1937 *China, Glass and Lamps* ad.

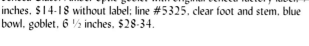

Seneca Glass. Amber optic goblet with original Seneca factory label, 7 inches, $14-18 without label; line #5325, clear foot and stem, blue bowl, goblet, 6 ½ inches, $28-34.

Streamline line, Seneca Glass Co. Design patent No. d 60637 Tumblers, Stigel green, 5 inches, $16-24; 4 inches, $18-22; 3 inches, $14-18; 2 inches (shot glass), $18-24.

Streamline line, Seneca Glass Co. Design patent No. d 60637. Tumblers, amber, 4 inches, $12-18; 3 inches, $10-16; 2 inches (shot glass), $12-20.

Streamline line, Seneca Glass Co. Tumbler, light green, $14-18; and pink, $14-18. 4 inches.

Streamline line, Seneca Glass Co. Tumblers, cobalt blue, 4 inches, $18-24; 2 inches (shot glass), $18-24; and amethyst, 2 inches (shot glass), $14-20.

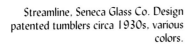

Streamline, Seneca Glass Co. Design patented tumblers circa 1930s, various colors.

Pitcher and tumblers, Seneca Glass Co. Ringed pitcher with applied reeded handle, 8 ¼ inches, $80-100; and streamline tumblers, 5 ½ inches. Note the use of a color and not crystal/clear applied handle. Most companies used clear for handles as Seneca may have at times.

No. 499. CORDIAL

No. 499. SHERBET

No. 499. FINGER BOWL

No. 499. GOBLET

No. 499. 6 oz. Ftd. TUMBLER

No. 499. SAU. CHAMP.

No. 499. COCKTAIL

No. 499. WINE

No. 499. PARFAIT

No. 30. CANDLESTICK

No. 12. 1" CONSOLE BOWL

No. 30. CANDLESTICK

SENECA GLASS COMPANY, MORGANTOWN, W. VA.

Seneca Glass Co. 1931 catalog Stemware line # 499, a shape widely used by Seneca, here with deep plate etching #633. Console bowl and candlestick with same etch.

Seneca Glass Co. 1931 catalog showing "Miscellaneous items in blue." It is cobalt, though it appears differently on these decades old tinted pages. Trim on these is etched and platinum "Naomi."

MISCELLANEOUS ITEMS IN BLUE WITH CRYSTAL TRIM DEC. P/D NAOMI

SENECA GLASS COMPANY, MORGANTOWN, W. VA.

Seneca Glass Co. 1930s stems include popular motifs like stacked rings. Wine shape #34, clear, 6 ½ inches, $16-24; and wine shape #156, clear, 5 ½ inches, $16-24.

Seneca Glass Co. elegant cut stemware in the manner which Seneca was famous for over the decades. Stem #1258 with unidentified cutting, 7 ¾ inches, $100-125. Stem #2258 with cutting #710 (note air trap bubble in stem near bowl), 7 inches, $70-90.

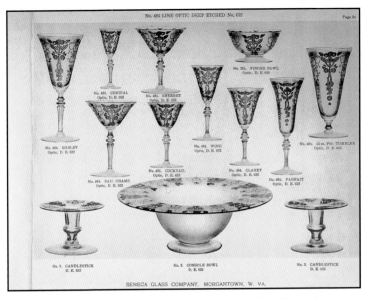

Seneca Glass Co 1931 catalog illustrates various decorating techniques including a luncheon plate in the plate etch, platinum decorated "Silvia."

Seneca Glass Co. 1931 catalog stylized Art Nouveau deep plate etching 632 on stem line #484. Note: console set with same etch and candle form #3, like shown above but flat top.

Rolled Edge Candlestick, Seneca Glass. Candlestick #30, Mushroom form, clear foot and ruby body, 3 ¼ inches tall, $70-90; cut similar to #1258, clear, 3 ½ inches tall, $50-70.

Seneca Glass. Ruby luster (color hand applied with brush then fired) wine, 5 ½ inches, $26-30; ruby luster saucer champagne or sherbet, 6 inches, $28-32; black foot and stem, clear bowl, wine, $24-28. Note that while looking similar in shape/pattern, the variances in bowl shape on similar stems would have created different line numbers for these at Seneca.

Handled wine, Seneca Glass. Amazing form that seems to have never become popular. Clear with hand cut flutes at juncture of bowl and stem. Original factory label. 6 inches. $35-45 without label.

Line 905, Seneca Glass Co. Sherbet/saucer champagne, clear foot and Stiegel stem, green bowl, 4 ¾ inches, $24-28; goblet, 6 inches, $32-36; and straight tumbler, 5 ½ inches, $14-20. Purchased as a wedding crystal set in the late 1930s.

Line 515, Seneca Glass Co. Frequently used "double hour glass stem" here as a Goblet with optic bowl cut #327, clear, 8 inches, $50-58; and wine cut #771 "Margery," 6 inches, $30-38.

Seneca Glass Co. Cigarette urn, clear foot and stem, cobalt urn, 7 ½ inches, $85-95. Gift to the author from Bob Page and Dale Frederiksen.

Line #498, Seneca Glass Co. Goblet, clear foot and stem, cobalt bowl, 7 inches, $45-50; wine, 5 inches, $28-35.

Seneca Glass Co. Various lines using ruby bowl shapes with the same clear "double hour glass stem" stem and foot. Oyster cocktail, 5 inches, $24-28; saucer champagne/sherbet, 5 inches, $34-38; wine, 4 ¾ inches, $32-36.

Seneca Glass Co. Double hour glass stem featuring crystal, cobalt and ruby bowls. Blue bowl wine, $28-35; clear goblet, $24-32; red saucer champagne, $34-38.

Lilly Pad Feet, Seneca Glass Co. Crystal bowl with various hand crimped "lily pad" feet. Ruby footed fruit or dessert bowl, 2 ¼ inches tall, $14-20; green footed tumbler, 3 inches tall, $12-16; black footed tumbler with original factory label, 5 ¾ inches, $16-20 without label; black footed tumbler with original factory label, 4 inches, $12-16 without label.

Line 903, Seneca Glass Co. All clear foot with Stiegel green bowl. Pilsner, 8 ½ inch, $35-42; tall tumbler, 6 ¾ inches, $32-40; juice tumbler, 3 ¾ inches, $18-24.

Line 903, Seneca Glass Co. Clear foot, amber bowl footed tumbler, 4 ¾ inches, $18-24; clear foot and tangerine tapered vase form, 8 inches, $45-60.

Line 903, Seneca Glass Co. Goblet, clear foot and stem, ruby bowl, 6 inches, $28-35.

Line 903 pilsners, Seneca Glass Co. All clear foot and colored bowls, 8 ½ inches. Stigel green, $35-42; ruby, $45-55; ruby luster, $35-45; cobalt blue, $45-55; light pale green, $30-36.

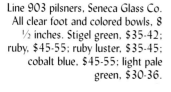

Line 903, Seneca Glass Co. All clear foot and stem with cobalt bowls. Pilsner, 8 ½ inches, $45-55; footed tumbler, 6 ¾ inches, $32-38; wine with dimple optic bowl, 4 ¼ inches, $28-34; wine, 3 ½ inches, $26-32; juice tumbler, 3 inches, $24-30; footed sherbet or bowl with dimple optic, 3 inches tall, $30-36.

Line #301, Seneca Glass Co. Green foot and stem wrapping around a clear bowl wine, 4 ¼ inches, $18-24; cordial, 3 ¼ inches, $24-30.

Seneca Glass Co. Variations in form. Brandy, clear, 4 ½ inches, $14-20; sherbet, cobalt foot and stem, clear bowl, original factory label, 5 inches, $24-32 (price without label); saucer champagne/sherbet, clear optic bowl with black foot and stem, 4 ½ inches, $24-30.

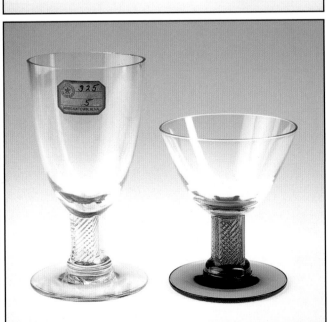

Line #325, Seneca Glass Co. Wine, all clear, 5 inches, $18-22; cordial, green stem and foot, clear bowl, 3 ½ inches, $ 35-42.

SENECA CRYSTAL
is the very
BEST—
"MADE IN AMERICA"

❧

BUYERS WILL FIND THE MOST COMPLETE LINE OF FINEST HANDCUT STEMWARE AND TABLE-WARE IN OUR SAMPLE ROOMS.

SENECA GLASS CO.
MORGANTOWN   W. VA.

SHOWROOMS

Phillips & Sammis, Inc., 1107 Broadway, New York, N. Y.; Ira A. Jones Co., 1545 Merchandise Mart, Chicago, Ill.; Howard S. Bokee, 122 W. Baltimore St., Baltimore, Md.

Seneca Glass Co. ad September 1937 from *China, Glass & Lamps* promotes one of the most popular and then moderately priced hand cut lines, Laurel.

Line 903, Seneca Glass Co. Laurel pattern hand cut footed tumblers, 6 inches, $22-28; 4 inches, $14-22.

Sang Bleu plate etching #30, Seneca Glass Co. Plate, clear, 8 ¾ inches, $35-42.

Sang Bleu plate etching, Seneca Glass Co. Liquor cocktail, clear, 5 inches, $18-24.

134

Seneca Glass Co. 1936 ad for plate etch "Bridal Bouquet," which is on the same stemware line as Seneca's Candlewick

Candlewick plate etching, Seneca Glass Co. All clear with green foot and stem. Sherbet, 3 ½ inches, $16-20; footed tumbler, 5 inches, $18-24; dessert or fruit bowl, 3 inches tall, $18-24.

Candlewick plate etching, Seneca Glass Co. Ruby footed, clear bowl footed sherbet, 3 ½ inches, $18-24; footed tumbler, 5 inches, $22-26; footed tumbler, 4 ½ inches, $20-24; clear footed tumbler with original factory "candlewick" label, 6 ¼ inches, $14-20 without label.

Bells, Seneca Glass Co. Large bell, cut #859, clear, 6 inches, $55-68; small bell, cut #660, 3 ½ inches, $25-35.

Seneca Glass Co. Selection of Seneca factory samples utilizing colored feet and clear bowls, all with original factory labels. Cobalt footed wine, 3 ½ inches; black footed ringed footed tumbler, 5 ¼ inches; ruby footed stem, 3 ½ inches. All $12-20 without labels.

Seneca 903 line, various elegant hand cuttings, oyster cocktail, 4 inches; goblet, 5 ¾ inches; oyster cocktail, 4 inches. No prices established.

Seneca Glass Co. Cut finger bowl, clear, with original factory label, $38-45.

Seneca Glass opaque green/jade footed tumbler with optic bowl and black lily pad foot, 5 ¼ inches, $45-65; goblet, Line 903, clear foot and stem with green opaque/jade and optic bowl, 6 inches, $60-70; wine, black foot and stem, Line 903, opaque green/jade bowl, 4 ¾ inches, $65-75.

Vitrolite

It is challenging to include an essay on a structural or architectural glass company for a collecting audience. However, Vitrolite makes that challenge easier.

It appears the story began in Parkersburg as early as 1909. In that year, Sanborn Fire Maps show a factory 3 ½ miles north of the Courthouse in Parkersburg entitled "The Meyercord-Carter Co. Mfgrs of Vitrolite Tile." Mapped in 1909 with a product line defined and shown in a 1908 photo now owned by the Manville Corporation (later owners of the factory), production likely began in 1908. So what was Vitrolite Tile?

Vitrolite is structural glass in slabs (sheets) from 5/16th to 1 ¼ inches thick. It combines the qualities and appearance of marble, glass, and ceramics. It came in white, ivory, jade, lavender, and black. Reports of red and other colors exist in worker's accounts. It was, as a 1921 Parkersburg Polk's Directory boasted, "Better Than Marble" due to its non-porous, unstainable qualities.

Local legend states that a Chicago sign manufacturer, George R. Meyercord, had been purchasing opaque (white) sheet glass from Opalite Tile Co., a Pennsylvania firm. He heard the glass manufacturer was considering acquiring decals and creating their own line of signs. He solicited some of the folks from Opalite to join him in creating a new company and white Vitrolite was born. Early decal work for advertising shows the products of this early time. An example of this ware that is well known and widely sought is an advertisement for I. W. Harper Whiskey. It appears as the front illustration in Regis and Mary Ferson's 1981 book Yesterday's Milk Glass Today. Other products were advertising sized "tiles" given away as paperweights.

In 1910 Meyercord-Carter Co. reorganized and the name became The Vitrolite Company. For decades to follow this was a factory in Vienna (a community adjacent to Parkersburg) and a company address of 133 West Washington Street, Chicago. In an elaborate fifty page catalog dated 1927 Vitrolite dealers were operating as Virolite Products Co., Vitrolite Manufacturing Co, or Vitrolite Construction Co., or some similar name and had twenty-six offices across the U.S., and one in Canada, Cuba, London, and Osaka, Japan. This was a quickly successful company.

A look at the catalogs' offerings is dazzling: lunch counters, cafeteria counters, soda fountains and back bars, tables, dresser and table tops, chairs, stools, coat hooks, and endless other accessories (foot rests, table shoes (?), etc.), Barber shop and Beauty parlor cases, installations and furniture, bakery shop and meat market refrigerators and installations, and architectural elements. These architectural elements included panels, pilasters, wall, and more. Special illustrations show Vitrolite used in hospitals, schools, and industrial settings. Many of these adaptations could be viewed at the company show rooms in Chicago. These rooms, maintained on the sixth floor of the Chamber of Commerce Building at Washington and LaSalle Streets include diversity from a Pompeian Room to a bathroom.

The glass was layered, carved, beveled, cut, etched, and had color added to the textured portions. In architecture, the St. Francis Church Clock Tower in Cincinnati, Ohio, was decorated with ornamental Vitrolite panels, seven by nine feet in size. In Washington, D.C., the Mayflower Hotel had cashier's stands, wall panels, and table tops with elaborate designs in Vitrolite. Vitrolite grills, featuring large cut away sections in amazing detailed geometric or nature scenes, such as deer in a wood lot, were included in a sun parlor in the Bricken home in New York and other places.

Examples of decorated ink well bases made for leading fountain pen manufacturers were part of the production. I have seen round decorative tiles, as for plants or hot dishes, etched to feature a highly stylized Art Nouveau female nude tucked gracefully to fit the circular Vitrolite. Square and rectangular tiles with etched designs can be found intended for the same purposes. Perhaps they were only made for local use, as glass house whimseys, but checker boards, lamp bases, ash trays, radio cases, and endless other applications of Vitrolite exist. In an excellent article capturing local recollections of the company, author Edelene Wood reports one story of Albert Travis, a graduate of Carnegie Institute in Pittsburgh, "who made lovely pink flamingoes on etched and sand blasted pieces." There are amazing pieces of Vitrolite out there waiting to be discovered. In neighborhoods near the factory, kitchens, bathroom, and other uses in the same manner as tile are not uncommon, as they must exist across the US and around the globe. A June 1929 ad in The House Beautiful, a very upscale magazine, has a full page advertisement for Vitrolite that begins "If I had a kitchen like that . . ." and showing two illustrations of Vitrolite in use. It was "the rage."

Exterior uses of Vitrolite are numerous and now being appreciated for their often Art Deco designs. Theater entrances, shoe store fronts, bank buildings, and more were given the classic look of black marble or the playful zing of colored Vitrolite.

By the 1930s additional colors included agates, cadet blue, sky blue, light gray, dark gray, jade, Alamo tan, red, peach, mahogany, cactus green, black, and white. In some creations various colors were laminated and cut away to expose layers of color. In 1935 Vitrolite had been acquired by Libbey-Owens-Ford, one of the giants in the flat glass industry. Libbey-Owens-Ford was the last producer of Vitrolite. By the 1950s, Vitrolite and all architectural glass was fading in popularity.

Note that Vitrolite, a major producer of flat architectural glass, was not, however, the only producer. Across the Ohio River, Marietta Manufacturing Co. produced Sani-Onyx and Sani-rox (perhaps their product name was a liability?); Pittsburgh Plate Glass marketed slabs of architectural glass called Carrara, named after a type of marble. Others around the US and world produced similar products.

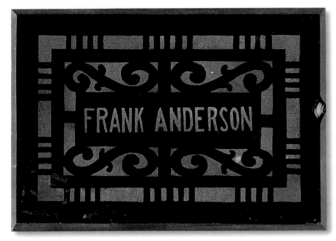

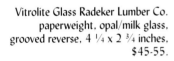

Virolite Glass paperweight, black, sand carved with the name "Frank Anderson," grooved reverse, 5 x 3 ¾ inches, $15-22.

Vitrolite Glass Knights Templer paperweight, opal/milk glass, grooved reverse, 3 x 4 ½ inches, $30-45.

Vitrolite Glass Radeker Lumber Co. paperweight, opal/milk glass, grooved reverse, 4 ¼ x 2 ¾ inches, $45-55.

Westite Glass

This company's story begins in Brilliant, Ohio, with a company that produced glass there before relocating to Weston, West Virginia. The firm, Brilliant Glass Products, is incorporated as a West Virginia corporation in 1927 and in bankruptcy by 1929. From the remains of the Brilliant Glass Co., new production came for a concern initially called Balmer-Westite Co. In June of 1930, Balmer-Westite becomes just Westite Company and production continued until the factory burns in 1936. J. H. Balmer of Trenton, New Jersey, was president of the company, which he capitalized originally to produce his patented line of glass bathroom fixtures. The products consisted of toothbrush holders, towel bars and holders, cup holders, etc. that mounted on the wall. Balmer had produced these same fixtures in china. Glass fixtures often bear the company name, patent information, etc. impressed into their reverse.

In addition to "slag" or marblized glass, Westite and its predecessors created light pink and green glass, sometimes found with a satin finish. The Westite line of solid opaque colors include a near jade green, light blue, black glass, and others.

It was plant manager John A. Henderson who seems to have created a line of glass jardinières, garden dishes, vases, and bowls. Henderson photographed these glass objects lovingly, setting them in and near his home as he compiled illustrations of the company products. The line, called Westite Ware, was marketed to florist company literature as "advanced glass pots for plants over porous clay pots whose walls sucked moisture away from plants, etc." In the early 1930s photographs, a strong eastern influence is shown in the use of the glass and flower arrangements.

Some of the moulds used as pansy bowls and ivy bowls may be recognized as the exact same mould used to create the bottoms to powder dishes found marked Ramsey's. Ramsey's was a cosmetic company that used Westite produced containers. Other pieces may be found with the word Westite in a bow-tie shaped logo and the words "Weston W.VA." beneath the logo or "Weston W.Va." above the logo and "Made in USA" under it. In a time when few glass producers marked their products, Westite can be found with several variations of company markings.

Other Westite customers were Woolworth, for whom glass flower pots were made bearing a Woolworth logo/monogram, and cold cream companies. Candle sticks, gear shift knobs, electric lamp parts, and stemmed compotes and cake stands can be found made by Westite or its predecessors. A photograph of an early truck decorated for a local Labor Day parade is a moving catalogue of Westite glass.

Locally the company has been called the "marble factory," giving rise to some intriguing questions as to the product line.

Family interviews, excavations at the site, and literature reviews confirm that "marble" in the case of Westite means marbled or slag glass, glass composed of varying colors swirled together and thus resembling (sometimes) marble.

After Westite burned, Henderson took some of the moulds to the Akro Agate Glass Co. in nearby Clarksburg, West Virginia, and they made glass for him, marketed as Westite, for a short time. Henderson and the moulds would shortly find a new home at Akro, where the moulds were altered over time and became the nucleus for a larger line of glass pots and garden dishes produced by and marked Akro Agate. Because of this connection and the visual similarities of Westite to some Akro Agate, collectors of Akro have made Westite a sought-after glass.

Westite cold cream jar, threaded top with black metal lid, $25-35; green slag cigarette jar with slag glass cap, 3 inches to top of jar, $35-45; jade green cold cream jar, threaded top with black metal lid and original paper labels, Estelle Cosmetics Co., Detroit, Michigan, $20-30 without label.

Westite Glass flower pots, 6 ½ tall, #300, $60-65; #302 "Westite" embossed on bottom, 5 inches tall, $30-38; #301 Westite embossed on bottom, 3 ¾ inches tall, $24-28; #300, 2 ¾ inches tall, "Westite" embossed on bottom, $26-30; #299, 2 inch tall, $38-42; 1 ¾ inches tall bottom embossed "souvenir WESTITE Weston, W.Va.," inside bottom of pot says "N.J. Flower Show Nov. 3 to 9," $75-85.

Westite coasters, clear embossed "Labor Day N.H. of A. F. G.W. U. 1928 L.U. No. 70 of North America Weston, W.Va. (graphic of clasped hands and glass objects)." Scarce, no price established, jade green, "Westite Made in West Virginia" and blue "Westite Made in West Virginia," 3 inches, $180-200.

Westite #299 slag ribbon rim decoration mini-pot, 2 ¼ inches, $38-42; jade panel flutes at base, 2 inches diameter, "A Z O" embossed in bottom. Uncommon. No price established.

Opposite page, bottom: Westite #650 Japanese planter, 11 ¼ inches length x 6 ¾ inches width, $300-600 depending on color

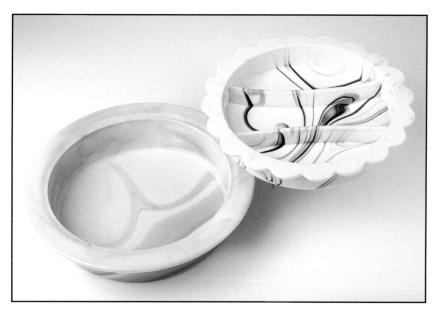

Westite rimmed slag garden dish, 2 ¼ inches x 10 inches diameter, $180-200; #600 slag divided 3 part garden dish, scalloped rim, rayed bottom, 1 ¾ inches x 9 inch diameter, $200-220.

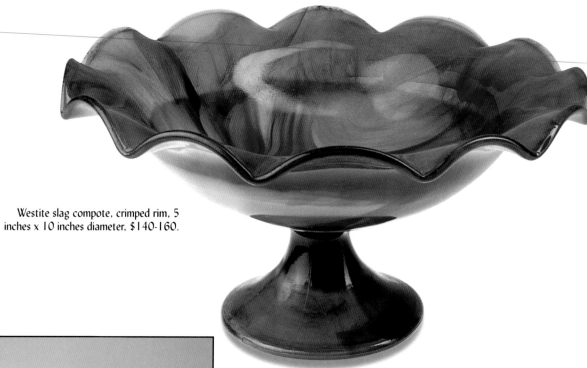

Westite slag compote, crimped rim, 5 inches x 10 inches diameter, $140-160.

Vases, Westite Glass. #312 Slag "flying buttress base," 8 ½ inches, $65-75; #315 ribbon rim trumpet form vase, 7 ½ inches, uncommon, $150-170; #311 black straight sided vase, 8 inches, $40-60; #310 slag, 6 ½ inches x 2 ¾ inches diameter, $40-60.

Westite #330 garden dish, 3 inches x 8 inches diameter; "green mottled," 2 inches x 7 inch diameter, $30-40.

Westite #321 "utility bowl," 8 ¾ inches at handles, $50-60; #651 scalloped rim, 4 inches tall x 8 ½ inches, $25-30.

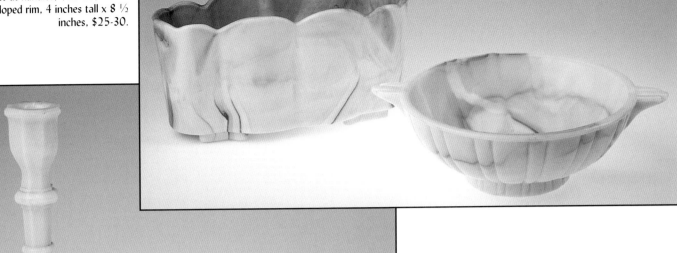

Westite single candlestick, black, satin pink, ivory, 3 ½ inches diameter, $22-28 depending on color. Note: this low shape is identical to Houze Glass products except Houze will always bear a mould number on the bottom. Back row: slag candlestick by Brilliant Glass (predecessor to Westite), octagonal, 8 ½ inches, No Price established; low stick six panel with floral pressed patterns, 4 ¼ inches, $22-28. Note: some of the low stick embossed under base, "Brilliant Weston W.Va."

Westite #140 Nasturtium bowl, 2 ¾ inches x 6 inches diameter, $20-28; three toed bulb bowl, "Westite" embossed bottom, 2 ¼ inches x 5 inches diameter, $25-35.

Westite #340 Nasturtium bowl with unfired factory hand painting, 2 ¾ inches x 6 inches diameter, crimped sided, #320 fern bowl, side crimped oddly at factory, three toed bulb bowl "Westite" embossed bottom 2 ¼ inches x 5 ½ inches. Both $22-32.

Westite covered powder dish, eight lobed dish, 5 ¼ inches diameter slag, $40-60; clear with satin finish, $35-45; black with gold decoration, $40-55.

Westite six sided "Ramses" shape. Ramses embossed on bottom of some but not all powder dish with lid, 4 ½ inches diameter x 2 ¼ tall without lid. Dark red with lid, scarce, no price established; jade green with lid, $65-80; Lilac opaque rimmed, never took lid, $45-55; slag, no lid, $40-50 without lid.

Westite #306 square with ribbon "jardinaire," 5 inches, "W" in diamond on base (possible for F. W. Woolworth stores), $32-38; #305 flared round ivory with factory hand painted decoration, 3 ¾ inches, $28-34; #314 narrow ledge vase (for windows or narrow ledges!), 4 ½ tall and 5 x 2 ½ inches at top, $35-45.

Westite bridge set with original box. Ivory, black, transparent pink, and jade green, 1 ½ x 3 inches, $140-160 with box.

Westite ash trays, slag ash tray with match book holder in center, 3 ¾ inches, jade green, embossed in bottom "Weston Service Station 1931 Fireman's Convention August 20-21-22," 4 inches, $100-120 each.

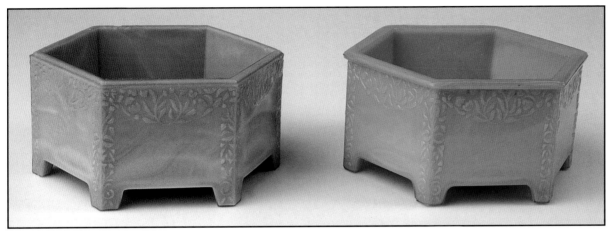

Westite opaque lilac six sided powder dish, embossed "Ramseys" on base and same mold with different rim, $45-55 without lid. Same mold and form becomes garden dish #360, which never had lid, shown here in opaque blue, $75-85. Note rim variances.

Westite #1000 six sided cream and sugar sets. Slag sugar, $18-24; transparent green sugar, "old rose" pink sugar, and old rose creamer, $12-15 each. 2 ¾ inches to top of handles.

Tumblers, Westite or Balmer – Westite (an early company name). Jade green, $30-40; and opaque blue, $30-40. 3 ¾ inches flute panels at rim, bottom embossed "Westite, Pat'd Weston, W.Va.", scarce, opaque Vaseline, no price established; and opaque blue, 3 ¼ inches, $12-18; transparent green with satin finish flute panels at base, 3 inches, $15-20; bathroom tumblers, slag rounded base, 3 ¼ inches, $25-28.

Westite pot trays or tiles, four individual feet, 6 inch square, $35-45; 3 ¾ inch square with pot ring and shown with bowl, $35-45 tray only; 6 inch square slag, $35-45.

Westite #317 slag tab handled vase, crimped top slag, $50-60; and jade green, $35-40. 6 ¼ inches.

Westite stacking bridge ash tray set, black, jade green, and transparent green. Embossed on bottom "Weston, W.Va. WESTITE Made in USA," 3 ¼ inches, $10-16 each.

Weston Glass Co.

Weston Glass Co. began operation in Weston, West Virginia, around 1913 in the factory that had been home to Bastow Manufacturing Co. (1909-1911) and then briefly leased to Travis Glass, a milk bottle manufacturer.

The new concern purchased the factory in 1919. In 1920 the owners of Weston Glass asked Louie Wohinc (see the Louie Glass story earlier in this volume) to take over management of the company. In 1931, at the height of the depression, Louie Wohinc accepted a single order for two thousand dozen tumblers per day for a year. It was such brilliant salesmanship that ensured the success of the interconnected local Louie glass concerns. Weston Glass was a part of the glass empire in Weston that reported in 1936 to be producing three boxcar loads of glass per day, roughly 15,000 dozen pieces per day, and employing over 1,200 people.

Weston Glass made rose and light green glass as well as colorless in its early years. The shapes are, in many circumstances, difficult to discern from other hand formed, mouth blown, paste mould glass houses products. Simple and elegant, the pieces bear no mould seams and are ideal for cutting or decorating. From the beginning glass made in Weston has surfaced on the market under the names of companies from New Jersey, New York, New England, and Chicago . . . plus points all over the globe!

Not all Weston Glass is seamless as some pieces were mouth blown in iron moulds, which impart a simple pattern and leave a tell tale seam where the two pieces of the "iron mould" met and closed.

In the summer of 1938 a Blackwell, Wielandy Company catalogue from St. Louis illustrates a Royal Blue (cobalt) 12 inch vase with platinum hairlines and edges. This is a Weston product amidst glass from other producers around the world.

A 1939 ad in the *China and Glass Directory* illustrates crystal stemware with black amethyst feet, including lily pad feet. Such were made at Weston Glass, or any of the Wohinc related companies in Weston.

The company's factory was destroyed by fire in June of 1932 and production ceased. A second Weston Glass Co. was formed several years later but should not be confused with this earlier company. This later concern's products were not in color and should not be mistaken for those of the earlier Weston Glass.

Hokey Pokey stemware, Weston and/or Louie Glass. Green with "hokey pokey" twist stem and unidentified gray hand cut rose decoration. Wine, 5 ¾ inches, $14-18; cordial, 5 inches, $18-22.

Footed tumblers, Weston Glass Co. Black foot and green optic bowl, $12-18; black foot and clear optic bowl, 5 inches, $8-12.

No. 905. 9 oz.
Goblet

No. 905. 6 oz.
Sau. Champ.

No. 905. 8 oz.
Sherbet

No. 905. 4½ oz.
Parfait

No. 905. 3 oz.
Wine

No. 905. 3 oz.
Cocktail

No. 300. 9 oz.
Goblet

No. 300. 6 oz.
Sau. Champ.

No. 300. 6 oz.
Sherbet

No. 300.
2½ oz.
Wine

No. 300.
3 oz.
Cocktail

No. 300. 12 oz.
Ftd. Ice Tea

No. 300. 12 oz.
Ftd. Ice Tea

No. 300. 10 oz.
Ftd. Tumbler

No. 300. 10 oz.
Ftd. Tumbler

THESE ITEMS CAN BE MADE IN ROSE, GREEN AND CRYSTAL IN STRAIGHT OPTIC, LOOP OPTIC AND DIAMOND OPTIC.

Weston Glass and Louie Glass catalog page. Stemware line #905 "banded ball" "hokey pokey" stem.

Parfait stem, Weston Glass Co. Green foot and octagonal stem, pink optic bowl, 6 ½ inches, $12-16.

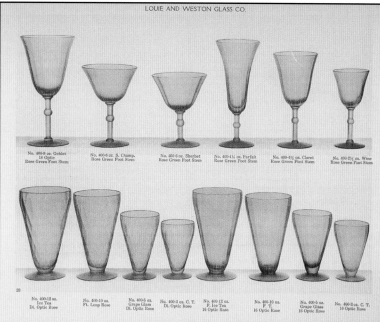

No. 400-9 oz. Goblet
Rose Green Foot Stem

No. 400-6 oz. S. Champ.
Rose Green Foot Stem

No. 400-6 oz. Sherbet
Rose Green Foot Stem

No. 400-4½ oz. Parfait
Rose Green Foot Stem

No. 400-4½ oz. Claret
Rose Green Foot Stem

No. 400-2½ oz. Wine
Rose Green Foot Stem

No. 400-12 oz.
Ice Tea
16 Optic
Di. Optic Rose

No. 400-10 oz.
Ft. Loop Rose

No. 400-5 oz.
Grape Glass
Di. Optic Rose

No. 400-3 oz. C. T.
Di. Optic Rose

No. 400-12 oz.
F. Ice Tea
16 Optic Rose

No. 400-10 oz.
F. T.
16 Optic Rose

No. 400-5 oz.
Grape Glass
16 Optic Rose

No. 400-3 oz. C. T.
16 Optic Rose

Weston Glass and Louie Glass catalog page. Stemware line #400 with six sided "hokey pokey" stem.

Weston Glass Co. Lily pad black foot and clear bowl with unknown gray hand cutting, 5 ½ inches, $14-18; clear #1108 jug with applied black handle and black lid, 9 inches to top of jug, $55-75. *Roy and Doris White collection.*

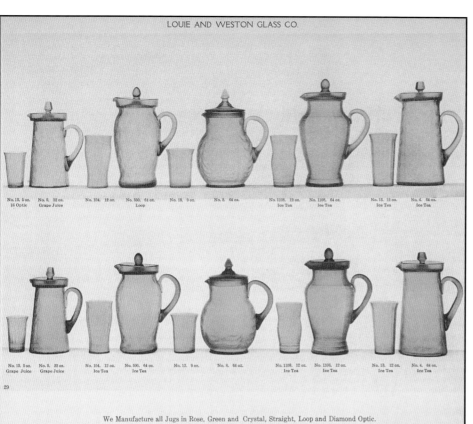

Weston Glass and Louis Glass catalog page. Jugs and tumblers galore.

Weston Glass and Louie Glass catalog page. This catalog appears to be circa late 1930s(?).

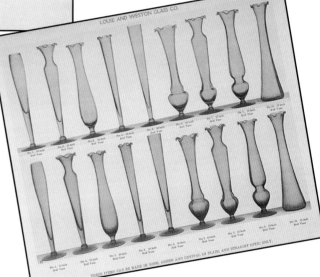

Weston Glass and Louis Glass catalog page. Bud vases. Compare to original catalog pages by Huntington Tumbler and others in this book for striking similarity.

Weston Glass and Louie Glass catalog page. Note: marmalade and jam jars are not the same!?

Weston Glass and Louie Glass catalog page. Tumble up or night sets consisting of water bottle and tumbler- lid. Style No. 1 and No. 2 continued in production as crystal clear products into the 1970s in Weston.

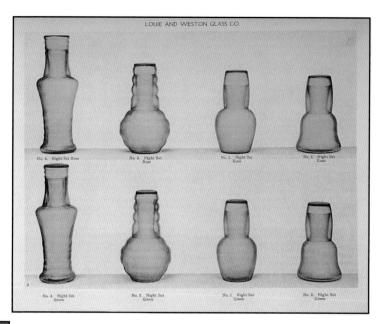

Popular stemware shapes from Weston Glass Co. and the other related Weston glass houses. Goblet, cobalt foot and colorless pulled stem, optic bowl, 7 ¾ inches, $16-22; clear 3 ringed and panel optic bowl with pulled stem gold banding decoration on rim and foot, 7 ¾ inches, $12-16. Both shapes of bowls appeared in area catalogs for decades with various stems and variations. Decoration probably by West Virginia Glass Specialty Co.

Weston Glass Co. pink sherbet, 3 ½ inches, sherbet with gray hand cutting, gray cutting being the unpolished cuts that are left to look "gray" and thus stand out against the smoother glass surface, 4 inches, $8-14; crimped bud vase, 10 inches, $12-16; iron mold imitation optic hour glass crimped vase, 8 inches (later produced as machine made by numerous others), $18-24.

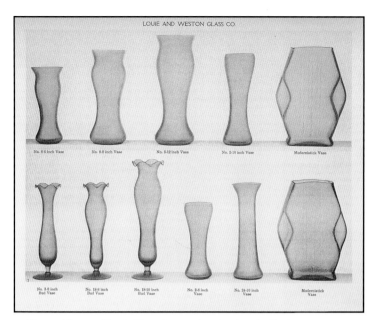

No. 8 6 inch Vase   No. 8-8 inch Vase   No. 8-12 inch Vase   No. 2-10 inch Vase   Modernistick Vase

No. 3-8 inch Bud Vase   No. 18-8 inch Bud Vase   No. 18-10 inch Bud Vase   No. 2-6 inch Vase   No. 24-10 inch Vase   Modernistick Vase

Weston Glass and Louie Glass Co. catalog showing the illusive "Modernistick vase." The West Virginia Museum of American Glass seeks this shape.

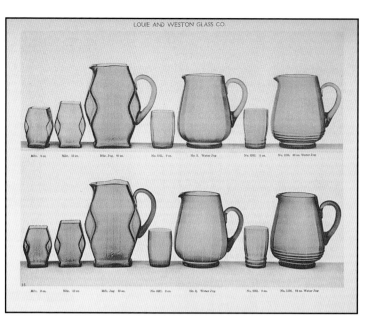

Mdc. 9 oz.   Mdc. 12 oz.   Mdc. Jug, 60 oz.   No. 6161, 9 oz.   No. 3, Water Jug   No. 6262, 9 oz.   No. 1206, 60 oz. Water Jug

Mdc. 9 oz.   Mdc. 12 oz.   Mdc. Jug, 60 oz.   No. 6467, 9 oz.   No. 3, Water Jug   No. 6262, 9 oz.   No. 1206, 64 oz. Water Jug

Weston Glass and Louie Glass Co. catalog showing jugs and tumblers. Note the "Mdc." Line is their Modernistick vase from the image above with a pulled spout and applied handle. Jugs #3 and #1106 are confusingly similar to jug shapes made also by others.

Weston and Louie Glass Co. Ring based #1106 jug shown in catalog page above, with drape optic, green, 7 inches, $35-50; green ringed tumbler, 7 ¾ inches, $8-12; jug #1108 with applied handle and lid, 9 ½ inches to top of jug, $75-90 with lid.

West Virginia Glass Specialty

One more of the Weston, West Virginia, glass factories successful in the 1930s-1940s era was West Virginia Glass Specialty. Opening in 1930, it operated until 1987. By 1938 it had between 300 and 400 employees, a sizeable concern. It continued to be a major and visible force in the glass market until the end.

It began with "Louie Wohinc and associates purchasing the idle plant of Interstate Window Glass" according to China, Glass and Lamp 5 September 1928, but plant refurbishing took time and production actually began in 1930. Here is the name of glass mogul Louie Wohnic again (see Weston Glass and Louie Glass), but his partners included some of the families that had been early and influential central West Virginia glass workers. Weber, Pertz, Kraus, Hager, and Ransinger were among this company's officers and provided leadership for decades to this company.

Production was diverse over time but it was often the hand decorating shops of West Virginia Glass Specialty that created the company's distinctive wares. In 1936 over 100 persons worked in the decorating shop alone. One of the first decorations introduced in the 1930s was a line of "ice decoration" where ground glass was fused to a completed glass object. By 1936 orange, blue, and crystal ice decorations were being produced. The ice decoration, reminiscent of nineteenth century overshot art glass in appearance and manufacturing technique, was called Glacial Glass and Frost Nip in later years of production. It continued in production for over four decades.

Color was also important in the first decade, but ceased to be produced in any large quantity in 1940. The 1931 China and Glass Directory listed all three interconnected Weston companies, Louie Glass, Weston Glass, and West Virginia Glass Specialty, in one advertisement and noted "Topaz, a brilliant new color: pink, green, crystal, and black offer a wide color range." An ad in China, Glass and Lamps of May 1936 notes the introduction of the new "Royal Blue," also called "Louie Blue" in the same ad! The addition of blue, bringing the color offerings to five, would complete the West Virginia Glass Specialty color prior to the conversion to crystal only in 1940.

One of the most popular of cocktail shakers of all times was made by West Virginia Glass Specialty in the 1930s. The ladies leg shaker is known in ruby, blue, and crystal with various decorations and is widely illustrated due to its novel shape and chrome strapped on high heel holder. Seldom is there mention of its West Virginia origin.

An image of a master decorator at this company appears as a large color photo in National Geographic issue of August 1940. Showing wonderful color, crystal, and hand painting, the photo likely dates from 1938 or 1939. This image gives a good visual introduction to the diversity of West Virginia Glass Specialty products at that time.

During World War II, trade journals reported West Virginia Glass Specialty "fulfilled huge Navy and Maritime Commission contracts" and thus survived to flourish in later decades before closing in 1987. It was one of several factories in Weston that contributed to the 2,000 plus employees here who engaged in producing glass and thereby allowing this small city to declare itself the Handmade Glass Capital of the World.

Marmalade jar #106, West Virginia Glass Specialty. Jar with spoon notched lid, cobalt/Ritz blue with platinum banding, 4 inches to top of jar, $38-48.

Vases #20, West Virginia Glass Specialty Co. Urn formed vase, clear with red luster and gold band decoration, $40-50. Cobalt blue with clear reeded handles, $60-80; both 9 ½ inches.

Vase, West Virginia Glass Specialty. Vase, cobalt blue with enamel advertisement for Weston Plaza Restaurant, $40-55; and undecorated black amethyst, $12-22. Also found decorated with "Souvenir The Grand Glass Exposition Sept. 5 – 8 – 1938 Weston W. Va." and other souvenir pieces. All 7 ¼ inches.

Vases, West Virginia Glass Specialty Co. Vase, cobalt blue with platinum bands, $45-65; ruby, both crimped tops, 11 ½ inches, $65-78. *Susie and John Determan collection.*

Vases, West Virginia Glass Specialty Co. Crimped top vase, clear satin and platinum band decoration, $35-45; black amethyst, $40-58; both 11 ½ inches.

Barbell Cocktail shakers #742/449, West Virginia Glass Specialty Co. Shaker, red with platinum band decoration, $150-220; cobalt blue, $140-200; both 11 ¼ inches to top of glass. This form remained in the catalog through the 1960s in clear.

Cocktail shakers, West Virginia Glass Specialty Co. "Long Feller" very tall shaker, so named in catalog, #741/10 cobalt blue with chrome top, 13 ¼ inches to top of glass, $140-200; same mold crimped circa 1937 as vase No. 741 in ruby, 13 inches, $75-85; and green Frost Nip with platinum bands and chrome top #4/840, 8 inches to top of glass, $70-85.

Decorated ruby, West Virginia Glass Specialty Co. Ruby glass production pre-summer of 1940. Footed tumblers, gold banded, 3 ½ inches; platinum banded, 3 inches; platinum banded small ringed tumbler, 2 ½ inches; footed ringed stem with platinum banding, 3 1/3 inches. All $8-14.

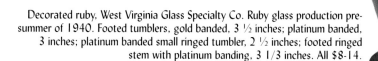

Candlestick and bowl, West Virginia Glass Specialty and Louie Glass Co. Candlestick, cobalt blue, 6 ¾ inches, $40-45 each; console bowl, clear foot and cobalt blue stem and bowl, 8 inches, $60-75; candlestick, ruby, 6 ¾ inches, $45-50 each. Made in clear, in "Ritz"/cobalt blue, in red, and with platinum decoration from West Virginia Glass Specialty.

Jugs, West Virginia Glass Specialty and Louie Glass Co. Cobalt blue three ring pitcher with attached chrome handle, $80-95; and #453 ruby with clear reeded applied handle, $90-100. Both 8 ½ inches to top.

West Virginia Glass Specialty Co. Vase with parrot and platinum band decoration, clear, 10 ½ inches, $24-34; plate, peacock decoration shown in circa 1930 catalog as "decoration D-84," clear, 8 inches, $14-18.

Bubble ball bowl, West Virginia Glass Specialty Co. Floral and band decoration, $20-28; ruby luster, $20-28; both 6 ¾ inches. *West Virginia Museum of American Glass collection.*

Ruby footed stem, West Virginia Glass Specialty. Line No. 37 sherbet with peacock decal decoration shown in undated company catalog in extensive 25 pieces offered in lines of stems, plates, serving pieces, and more. 3 ½ inches, $14-18.

Punch Bowl Set, West Virginia Glass Specialty Co. Punch bowl, under plate, and handleless cups. Company catalog number 400/400 for bowl, plate, and six cups. Here with Decoration D-84. Clear Frost Nip over floral decals with platinum banding. Plate 10 ¾ inches. Set with 8 cups, $200-250. Susie and John Determan collection.

Plate, West Virginia Glass Specialty Co. Clear plate with multicolored decal, Frost Nip decoration over decal on rim and platinum band. Shown with decal and platinum but not frost nip in a 1920-30s catalog as a "crystal pie set" including cream, sugar, cups and saucers, tow handled serving plate, and dessert plates. 6 ½ inches, $18-20.

Vase #105, West Virginia Glass Specialty Co. Ruby with clear foot vase, $38-48; cobalt blue foot with crystal body vase and floral and platinum band decoration, $40-45; both 11 inches. Made in Ritz blue with clear foot and noted in 1937 as new in that combination in a trade journal ad. See also Queen Alfreda throne glass in Louie chapter.

Decorated tumblers, West Virginia Glass Specialty Co. Ringed base, black silhouette pixie silk screen over Frost Nip decoration, 4 ½ inches, $18-24 each.

Hourglass cocktail glass, West Virginia Glass Specialty Co. Clear with sham bottoms, green Frost Nip and platinum banding, 4 ¾ inches, $14-20; clear with clear Frost Nip and platinum banding, 3 ¼ inches, $12-18; clear with orange Frost Nip and platinum bands, 4 ¾ inches, $14-18.

Candy jar, West Virginia Glass Specialty. "Ritz" or cobalt blue with platinum bands and lid, $45-55; orange Frost Nip and platinum bands with lid, $35-45. Note the variances in shape. Over time Weston companies offered dozens of similar but slightly varying forms.

Frost Nip decanters, West Virginia Glass Specialty Co. No. 8 form with Blue Frost Nip and platinum decorations exactly as shown in circa 1930 catalog, 10 ½ inches to top of decanter, shown in 1920s era catalogs, $60-85; green Frost Nip and platinum decoration No. 2 decanter in same factory catalog, 9 ¼ inches to top of decanter, $40-60.

Tumble-ups, West Virginia Glass Specialty. Tumble-ups or night bottles. Bell shaped No. 2 bottle with tumbler, red Frost Nip and gold band decoration; bell shaped No. 2 bottle, blue Frost Nip and platinum band decoration; bell shaped No. 2, cobalt blue bottle with no tumbler shown as cap; No. 1 bottle cobalt blue and ruby, bell shaped No. 2. All $40-65.

Cocktail shaker, West Virginia Glass Specialty. Ruby with chrome stiletto shoe and lid. One of the most recognized of all shapes made in the Weston area factories. 12 ½ inches to top of glass, $1,000-1,400. Also found in clear with satin and commemorative decorations.

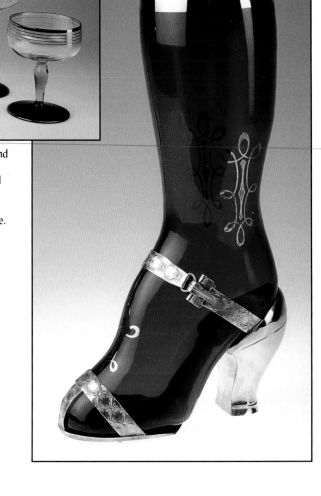

West Virginia Glass Specialty, "golden glow' decoration. Amber stain, black painted foot and platinum bands. Wine, 5 ½ inches, $12-16; goblet, 7 ¾ inches, $15-18; tumbler, 4 ¾ inches, $12-14; dessert plate, 6 ½ inches, $10-14; shot glass, 2 ¼ inches, $14-18; small tumbler, 3 ¾ inches, $10-14; luncheon plate, 8 ¼ inches, $14-18; saucer champagne/ sherbet, 5 ½ inches, $12-14; sherbet, 4 ¼ inches, $12-14. This set represents significant hand decorating and thus cost. It might have retailed in a department store or jewelry store.

"New for 1939" ad appearing in *China, Glass & Lamps* with an illustration captioned "Decorated lines . . . from West Virginia Glass Specialty Company."

Topaz color, West Virginia Glass Specialty or Louis Glass Co. goblet with gray hand cutting, 7 ¼ inches, $14-20; sherbet or saucer champagne, optic bowl with gray hand cutting, 5 ¼ inches, $12-16. Both possibly cut at one of several nearby Weston cutting/decorating shops.

West Virginia Glass Specialty Co. Woodland decal decoration, tall clear jug with applied handle illustrated in trade journal ad as shown above "new for 1939," 10 ½ inches, $65-85; tumbler, 5 ½ inches, $12-15. *Susie and John Determan collection.*

West Virginia Glass Specialty acorn form vase for hanging or fitting into metal wall bracket, green, 2 ½ inches, $8-12; trumpet vase, satin with gold and blue banded decoration, 12 inches, $35-45.

West Virginia Glass Specialty. Decal decorations jewel "hokey pokey" stem with hunt scene, 6 inches, $24-28; tumbler with 1930s era football player, 3 ¼ inches, $14-22.

Jug and tumblers, West Virginia Glass Specialty Co. Colorless ringed shape with Frost Nip and blue banded and hand cut gray decorations. Pitcher, 7 ½ inches, $60-75; tumblers, 3 ½ inches, $12-14.

Index

A

Akro Agate Co., 7, 8, 140
Alley Glass Co., 7-9
Alley, Lawrence E., 7-8

B

Balmer-Westite Co., 140
Bastow Manufacturing Co., 147
Beaumont Glass Co., 10-14
Beaumont, Percy J., 8
Blenko Glass Co., 15-16
Bonita Art Glass Co., 17-18
Brilliant Glass Products, 140

C

Canfield, Richard A., 10
Central Glass Works, 19-32
Columbia Glass Co., 33
Commercial Glass Co., 33
Co-Operative Flint Glass Co., 19
Cumberland Glass Works, 63

D

Dunbar Glass Co., 34-45

E

Economy Tumbler Co., 89
Economy Glass Co., 89
Empire Glass Co., 108

F

Fenton Art Glass Co., 46-51
Fostoria Glass Co., 52-56

G

GlassWorks WV, 69

H

Hazel Atlas Glass Co., 57-62
Heintzelman, H. L., 79

Henderson, John A., 140
Hobbs, Brockunier Co., 17, 19
Huntington Glass Co., 69
Huntington Tumbler, 63-68

I

Interstate Window Glass, 152

J

Jaeger, Otto, 17-18, 123

K

Kingwood Glass Co., 7
Kizinski, Stanislaus, 121

L

Lancaster Glass Co., 80
Lewis County Glass Co., 69
Louie Glass Co., 69-77, 78, 152
Ludwick Glass Co., 69

M

Mid-Atlantic Glass Co., 69, 78
Monongah Glass Co., 6, 79-88
Morgantown Glass Works, 89
Morgantown Glassware Guild, 89-97
Moulds, William, 79

N

New Martinsville Glass Co., 98-107
Northwood, Harry, 8
Northwood, H, Glass Co., 6

P

Pacquet Glass Co., 7
Paden City Glass Co., 108-120

Paramount Glass Co., 121-122
Pennsboro Glass Co., 7, 69
Princess House Glass, 69

R

Rochester Glass Works, 79

S

Seneca Glass Co., 123-137
Star City Glass Co., 121

T

Turner Glass Co., 80
Travis Glass, 147

U

Union Stopper Co., 8, 10

V

Viking Glass Co., 98
Vitrolite Co., The, 138-139

W

Wellsburg, WV, 5
Westite Glass Co., 140-146
Weston Glass Co., 69, 147-151
West Virginia Glass Specialty Co., 69, 152-159
White House glass, 89
Window glass, 5
Wismach Glass Co., The Paul, 108
Wohinc, Louie, 69-70, 147, 152
Wohinc, Margaret, 70

Z

Zilhman, Anthony, et al., 63